# *Splat!*

A Memoir

by

Adele Irving

Adele!

ISBN 9798583077465

# Dedication

This book has been a labor of love and a test of my courage. It is dedicated to eight incredible women in my life who have become a tremendous inspiration to me.

"Strong women aren't simply born. They are made by the storms they walk through."

Linda Lundstrom

Lia Keeping

Paulette Couture

Merle Nicholds

Jeannette Wheeler

Carol Fines

Erin Schonert

and

Audrey Hawkins

With a very special thank-you to
Tracy Quinton
for planting the seed so
many years ago.

# Foreword

Every person has a story. This is mine.

I'm a prairie girl. I can't even begin to count how many times I have driven west across the Canadian prairies. I find beauty in the flat, agricultural fields of Saskatchewan and the rolling hills of Alberta. I plan my stops. Wherever there's a Tim Hortons there's a washroom, and coffee to fill up before the next town. One thing for certain, you can't avoid the bugs hitting your windshield, especially just before dusk and more often after the first of August. I can remember more than once having to pull over to actually scrape the remains off the windshield so I could see to go further. So, when I was planning to write this book, its title came years before the pen was put to paper.

They say that art imitates life and life imitates art. Can you imagine my shock when I actually heard that someone else understood the title of my book and the feeling that life can go splat like a bug on the windshield? That visual was being broadcast by the CBS network across North America.

In the summer of 1974, I was a new mother at home with nothing to watch on TV but President Nixon's resignation. One day that August, a friend asked me if I watched *The Young and the Restless,* but I had never heard of it. I soon learned that it was a soap opera seen Monday to Friday and that my friend's brother, a Canadian actor, had a leading role. I began watching it to see her brother. His character was killed off right away, but forty-six years later I am still hooked on that TV show.

On Tuesday, May 11, 2011, one year after I wrote the first chapter and four years after deciding on the book's title, a conversation between the actors portraying Kevin and Chloe came up on *The Young and the Restless*:

Chloe says: "Okay, why can't we just be a normal couple? You know, I would even settle for a boring, normal couple that just sits there on the sofa and stuffs their faces with junk food every night. But, no, that's not us. It's not us at all. We're like this windshield that's bombarded with bugs and large windshield wipers. Like, splat—Jana. Splat—Angelo. Splat—Billy. You know, why can't we just, I don't know, pull into a full-service station that, uh, squeegees away all the stress?" (Sighs)

There you have it, I thought. Confirmation from a higher power, the writers at CBS. I must be on the right track!

# Chapters

1 – A Bug on the Windshield of Life .................................................................. 1

2 – Cops and Robbers ................................................................................... 9

3 – All in the Family ...................................................................................... 13

4 – Finding a Solution .................................................................................... 16

5 – Right Under My Nose ............................................................................... 21

6 – Nothing Changes if Nothing Changes ........................................................ 25

7 – Archie's Bunker ....................................................................................... 27

8 – Happy Anniversary ................................................................................... 29

9 – Too Hot to Handle ................................................................................... 31

10 – Skid Row ............................................................................................... 34

11 – The Secret Behind the Secret ................................................................. 37

12 – I Have a Secret Too ................................................................................ 40

13 – On My Own ........................................................................................... 42

14 – Breaking Point ....................................................................................... 47

15 – One More Time ...................................................................................... 49

16 – Parent Trap ............................................................................................ 52

17 – Saying Goodbye ..................................................................................... 56

18 – Therapy ................................................................................................. 61

19 – Searching for an Answer ......................................................................... 65

20 – Life Changing ......................................................................................... 68

21 – Suspicion and Solution ........................................................................... 70

22 – A Miracle of my Own ............................................................................. 72

23 – Millennium ............................................................................................. 74

24 – Hanging on for Dear Life ........................................................................ 78

25 – The Eye of the Tiger ............................................................................... 84

26 – Happy Crappy Birthday ........................................................................... 87

27 – Counting Down ...................................................................................... 89

28 – 11:52 p.m. ............................................................................................. 92

29 – Moving Life Forward................................................................95

30 – And So it Began ...................................................................101

31 – Pack Your Bags ....................................................................105

32 – Spooky Shit ...........................................................................109

33 – Truckload ..............................................................................114

34 – Angels Are with Me ..............................................................119

35 – This Too Shall Pass ..............................................................123

36 – Dipping My Toe in the Water ...............................................126

37 – My Top 10 List......................................................................128

38 – Geoff Smith...........................................................................132

39 – I See Dead People .................................................................135

40 – Walker...................................................................................138

41 – Making my Move...................................................................141

42 – Hotel Adele ...........................................................................144

43 – A Cast of Characters ............................................................147

44 – Catch and Release .................................................................153

45 – End of an Era ........................................................................156

46 – A Teenage Crush, Crushed ...................................................162

47 – It Sucks to be an Optimist ....................................................172

48 – You've Got One Chance to Make a First Impression............176

49 – Audrey Isabella......................................................................186

50 – She Sells Real Estate from the Other Side ............................191

51 – It's not a Pebble, it's a Rock.................................................199

52 – Grandpa and Grandma Get Married .....................................202

53 – My Happily Ever After Chapter ...........................................205

54 – You Can't Predict a Miracle.................................................210

# Splat!

"Most hearts of any quality are broken on two or three occasions in a lifetime.
They mend, of course, and are stronger than before, but something
of the essence of life is lost at every break."

—Robertson Davies, *Leaven of Malice*

## 1 – A Bug on the Windshield of Life

I believe that nothing in life is a coincidence and that I am simply turning the pages of my story and walking the path some greater power has planned. Did I know what the future held for me? Of course not. Sometimes I wish I did, simply so I could duck. Would I know when my life was half over? Perhaps not. My mom lived until she was ninety-one and maybe I will too. I do think that by the time you're halfway through your life you should know what you want and where you're going, with a destination in mind. For me, at the age of forty-four, I not only knew where I was going and what I wanted, I had everything I'd ever dreamed about. That was about to change forever. I didn't see it coming, because sometimes you're the bug and sometimes you're the windshield.

I was never an academic. Learning was not even on my list of priorities, simply because I wasn't being taught what I thought I needed to learn. At sixteen I asked my parents to send me to a private Catholic school. I thought at a religious school, if I prayed and the nuns prayed maybe my grades would improve. They never did. At my initial interview Sister Anselm, the school principal, expressed her concern. She felt I was too much of a social butterfly to fit in and achieve good grades. Fortunately for me enrolment was low and the school needed tuition, so I was accepted to St. Benedict's Academy, where I became the school's Social Director for two years. I was genetically predisposed to be a hospitable butterfly.

Something happened in my second year at St. Ben's. One day at our school assembly Sister Anselm called me on to the stage and asked me to twirl in front of the entire school. As I did, she announced that she wanted everyone in the all-girls school to look exactly like me because I was always "as neat as a pin." This would be unheard of in today's high school climate and it wasn't even cool in the late '60s.

The school closed a few years later, and ten years after my graduation we had a reunion of our class, which consisted of only thirteen girls. Early in the evening I found myself in the ladies' washroom standing in front of a sink and washing my hands beside Sister Anselm. She didn't even look like a nun anymore and was dressed in a simple polyester pantsuit. This gave me a golden opportunity to speak to her about that embarrassing spotlight she had put me under, so many years before. She stopped me in my tracks with an instant apology, explaining that the moment those words left her mouth she knew she'd made a mistake.

That's when I told her the truth. "Sister, what you said never upset me because everyone knew just what I was like. I was really no different than anyone else. My socks were full of holes, and I never took my blazer off because the armpits of my blouses were all ripped. The hem of my skirt was held up by masking tape and my buttons were held on by safety pins. I was the picture of perfection because I could pull it off, but underneath, I was no different than every teenage girl."

We really had a good laugh about that! But, all these years later I realize Sister Anselm had more insight into my true self than I did. At seventy years of age I still try to be the picture of perfection. You'll never see me looking unkempt or without a matching outfit and accessories and makeup. Sadly, I wear my perfection like armor and too many times chaos has hovered just below the surface.

When the new year of 1995 was rung in, I thought my life was perfect. I was living my dream and the best year of my life was unfolding. I had everything any woman could wish for: a wonderful husband, two beautiful children, a home, a career, and excellent health. I had been married to Dennis for twenty-four years. Life had never been better. He was the man of my dreams, incredibly handsome, funny, and generous. I loved him like crazy. We had been in our dream home for ten years—a 3400 square foot house decorated to perfection on three quarters of an acre backing onto a river, and we were mortgage-free. We were financially stable, and business was booming. These were the gravy years.

Our children, who were nineteen and twenty-one, had never given us, as parents, any grief. Damien, our son, was attending the University of North Dakota, and was planning to change his major. The Canadian dollar had dipped, so instead of school he spent the winter working for his dad and earning some of his tuition. Keele, our daughter, had been working for a year. It would take her longer to figure out where she was going, but soon, we would see her graduate with the first of her three degrees.

Nine years earlier in 1986, I had gone to work in the family business giving up the part-time airline job I loved so much. In 1974 when we bought the family taxidermy business from my parents, part of the deal was that I would never work at "the shop." I had lived with it all of my life and would never make the choice to be involved on a day-to-day basis. I had seen what it had done to my parent's marriage and didn't want that to happen to mine. However, by 1985 I didn't have a choice because my husband needed my help. One of our best friends had died of a heart attack at the age of forty and it scared Dennis. He asked me to come in part-time for a few months just to learn what was going on in the office. In case he had a premature death, he didn't want the staff to take advantage of me.

Simple enough, I thought. I would learn soon that things in the office were very wrong. About six months after I started, Dennis was on a business trip to Denver. I called him and said, "Someone has to go, it's either her or me, you choose." I was talking about our office manager who had been with us for twelve years. I learned that the staff hated her, and our customers couldn't stand her either. It was all about control and she wouldn't give an inch. We paid her off and let her go. That is how I found myself working there until 1993. Seven years of hell!

Working over forty hours a week, I often would go into the building at 6:00 a.m. to get a head start, as we were extremely busy. Everything about being there was against my nature. I'm not an office person. Not one to sit still for any length of time, I'd never seen a computer and my typing skills hadn't been used since grade eleven. At first, I thought it would be fun to have a place to wear all of the clothes in my closet. I would quickly learn that Dennis didn't want me to look too good. If I was wearing an expensive wardrobe, we would look too successful and the staff would want raises. He was weird about things like that. For months, after I got my new Mustang convertible, I would have to park it down the street so no one could see me pull up. And, no matter how cold a Winnipeg winter got, I could never wear my mink coat to work, for the same reason. Over time, I would become frumpier, dumpier and grumpier. Not a happy woman and certainly not a happy wife. At the end of the day, we had nothing to talk about except the business. We lived and breathed work. Many, many days I would cry all the way home. Friends advised me to quit, just walk out. You can't walk out when you actually own the company. I did not want to be there, so in order to leave the family business I needed to find something to replace it.

In the fall of 1992, I was invited to one of those direct-sales home parties, which was certainly nothing I was interested in. I didn't want to go but I appreciated an evening out. In the end I really enjoyed myself. The theme was fashion, and the products were clothing. I had been a clotheshorse all my life and this company suddenly had my attention, particularly because it was Canadian. The clothes were mix and match, affordable and washable. The price point was perfect. I went home with a brochure and kept the midnight oil burning as I pored over every detail, wanting everything they sold. A few weeks later, I went to another show and offered to help the fashion coordinator so I could get a feel for what was going on. It was now mid-October, and I would take a great deal of time thinking about this as an option to get out of "the shop."

By the first of December, I had made my decision and signed on the dotted line. Dennis said, "What the hell are you doing?" and friends couldn't figure why I would want to sell clothes door to door.

Of course, that is not what I would be doing. My plan was to buy my clothes so I could have everything they carried, at a discount, and sell just enough to pay off my credit card each month. I also planned a trip to Toronto in February to attend their national conference and check them out. I was always suspicious of direct-sales companies like this and I wanted to make sure they were not religion-based. If these were a bunch of "born agains" I would run for the hills. I did make the decision to invest some money into this new venture, $1900. I wanted to have every size and color. You have to spend money to make money. I learned that from my husband.

February 1993 came, and I arrived at the Regal Constellation Hotel in Toronto, filled with trepidation. The fashion show took place the first evening in the main ballroom. What was I doing? I started second guessing myself and the What-ifs started playing with my brain. What if I hated the clothes? What if no one would buy from me? What if I had wasted all this money? What if I was making a fool of myself? I was a nervous wreck.

My "sales manager" had arranged for me to room with someone I had never met before. We had to hurry as there would be a large and anxious crowd. Seats were on a first-come basis. I wore my very best dress: A little green plaid number with a dropped waist and a large white pinafore collar. The collar was wrinkled, and I didn't have time to order an iron to the room so in the dim light I used my hair dryer hoping the heat would straighten out the wrinkles. Well, it did more than that. It scorched the dress. Panic, absolute panic. I had ruined the dress. In fact, I would never be able to wear it again. Time was running out. I covered the scorch with my name badge. Then my earring broke, the one that matched the dress, and to add insult to injury, I put my fingernail through my pantyhose. It was a disaster.

I was feeling rushed and this was supposed to be fun? Outside the ballroom hundreds were standing in line impatiently waiting to get in and find the best seat. Once the doors opened, there was a pushing and shoving crush of women. My manager and the coordinator from Winnipeg waved at me to join them but I said no. I wanted to sit alone, alone in my misery at the front of the room near the stairs to the stage.

I could see everything from that point, and I could exit fast. There must have been over twelve hundred estrogen- and adrenaline-filled former homemakers who were now in business. The music pumped and the strobe lights flashed like lightning bolts. The women were on their feet screaming and then the curtain went up.

It was over too quickly, in a blur of color, sound and light. Then someone called my name. I was up and on to the stage in a flash, not fully realizing what was happening. Maybe this was the fateful reason I had chosen a seat so close to the stage. I would soon learn that I had won a prize. Everyone attending who had invested in their spring samples had their name in the draw, and it was my name they picked. What did I win? Nineteen one-hundred-dollar bills. My entire investment back! The crowd was cheering because in the past draws, the winners had invested very little, only a couple of hundred dollars as they were waiting until they had seen the collection. With the cash clutched in my hand, I was handed a microphone and was asked, "Would you like to say a few words?" So, there I was, overwhelmed and out of breath, wearing the wrong earrings, a giant run up my leg, and covering the scorch on my $300 dress was my large plastic name badge precariously perched, tilted and almost twirling there at the tip of my right breast.

I remember clearly what I said: "You are looking at a woman in a midlife crisis. I simply came to check you out. I don't know what a booking is or what a hostess does, but I think this is a sign from above that I am supposed to be here." There you have it. I was the one who had suddenly found religion.

This was the beginning of a marvelous adventure for me. For the rest of the conference everyone came up to meet me or rub my shoulder for good luck because they all thought I had luck on my side. On my flight home, I took my boarding pass and wrote, "Diamonds for me in '93." That was my goal. I quit working in the family business in April, then really got off my butt in May. Dennis phoned me at home one morning and asked if I could come in to help with the year-end paperwork. I couldn't do it. I knew that would be my pattern for life. He would always find a reason to get me back to the shop. Instead, I really got to work on my new career. Fear is a great motivator. By December 31st I had sponsored a team of eight women and sold over $55,000, which earned me my first prize, a diamond bracelet. Life had become all about setting goals and reaching them. At the company conference the next year, my boarding pass read, "Manager and more in '94." Coincidentally, I sat in the very same seat on the plane both years. But I believe nothing is coincidence.

So, flash forward to February of 1995 when my life couldn't have been more wonderful. Dennis accompanied me to our annual conference so that he could see what I had accomplished. My boarding pass goal had come true. I was the company's first sales manager in the city. I sold over $76,000 in twelve months, putting me in the top twenty-five of the company in Canada. At that time there were approximately five thousand women working for the company. I was also third in sponsoring for the year, having added twenty-three women to my own personal team. This made me a top money earner in team building month after month. I wasn't just on a roll—I was flying high—but, I was completely burned out, and I wrote on my boarding card one last time, "Stay alive in '95." I had no idea where that came from or how true it would become.

We returned home from the conference to a whirlwind. Having missed time at the office, Dennis worked late on Valentine's Day, which was the following Tuesday, and for the first time ever, he didn't even mention it. I supposed we would celebrate on the upcoming weekend. The weekend after that we would be going to Kananaskis, a Rocky Mountain resort in Alberta. This was part of a company reward for my hard work. It would be the first of many trips that would eventually take me to fabulous places in the world as a million-dollar manager.

On Thursday, February 16, 1995, Dennis and Damien came home from work around 4 p.m. Dennis had a fist full of movies he had rented on the way home. Damien was in his bedroom. Dennis was in the family room and I was upstairs in our bedroom watching Oprah. Suddenly I heard a very loud crash. Damien screamed, "Call 911, Dad's having a heart attack!" I rushed to the back door and into the closet to push the alarm buttons on our home security system. I thought I was summoning an ambulance and didn't know that it would be the police and the fire department who would answer the call. I started to run downstairs, but Damien yelled from the bathroom for me to stop. "Don't come down here, it's terrible. Go and get help!" Dennis was having a seizure. I opened the front door and ran across the street to find our neighbor Phyllis, who was a nurse. I pounded on the door, but no one was home. "Don't let him die," I pleaded with God as I ran barefoot through the snowbanks, down the driveway and across the street and then back again. I did not feel the subzero Winnipeg winter on my bare feet, for I was numb all over. "Don't let him die!" Dennis was foaming at the mouth and Damien was trying to restrain him. I wanted to go downstairs but I was in a complete panic because help wasn't coming. I tried to phone out, but when I pushed the alarm button it canceled the phone lines. I was terrified and I could hear terror in my son's voice too.

Finally, after what seemed like an eternity, I heard sirens in the distance. Dennis was coming around. A giant goose egg was rising on his forehead and creeping into his left eye. We didn't know what had happened. Did he trip on a bathmat and hit his head? Did he have a seizure and then fall? Was it a heart attack or a stroke?

As the sirens came closer down our mile-long street, I was out of my mind with fear. Damien called me into the bathroom and pointed to where his father had fallen. Then, as time stopped, and the police and firemen entered the house and came down the stairs, we had the answer. With the impact of a head-on collision, our lives changed forever. On the floor, we found a syringe. My husband was a drug addict.

Splat!

## 2 – Cops and Robbers

On that cold Thursday in February 1995, I followed closely behind the ambulance to the hospital, which was only about three miles from our home. Our daughter was born there. I'd had two surgeries there and had spent many, many hours in emergency with cuts, bumps, and the broken bones that go with raising a family. It was a safe place. In my mind it was a place to get fixed and to heal. They would make things right.

Inside the ER two big, burly Winnipeg cops were waiting for me and asked me to step inside a room with them. It was small and I felt like I was stepping into a closet. I am so claustrophobic and could feel the walls closing in on me. I don't remember being asked to take a seat. They just wanted answers. Who were our friends? What was Dennis's drug source? They wanted names, places, dates and times. Were they talking to me? There must be some mistake, some horrible mistake. My husband was not an addict. Bums on the street were addicts. The ER downtown at the Health Sciences Centre was for addicts, not this hospital in my neighborhood, upper-middle-class suburbia. That didn't happen here, and this wasn't happening now. I would soon learn that it doesn't matter who you are or where you come from, drug addiction can strike anyone. Addiction has no boundaries.

I couldn't even speak, but I remember thinking, "If my husband is a drug addict, then the queen is a hooker, and the pope is her pimp." This nightmare had to end. I wanted to wake up now. The two cops finally gave up. I am sure they realized that I was in shock. I knew they were just doing their job, but I was convinced they were so, very, very wrong about this.

This wasn't the first time I encountered the police force. Long before, something equally horrific had happened. It was the fall of 1973. Dennis and I had been married for two years and loved life in our first little bungalow. On a cold morning in October our family business was broken into. In the early morning, Dennis got the call and rushed down to our new building. We were the largest taxidermist in Canada at the time. On this particular October day burglars had smashed the front showroom windows, reached in and hauled off fourteen mounted polar bear rugs which were folded and stored in bags just under the window. We had just moved into our building and in the confusion of a move, we soon learned that the insurance for the building and its contents had not been transferred to the new location. At that time, we had not installed our security system and we were a prime target.

Using the phone lines, the police set up an alarm system for us. This would be sufficient until the new system could be installed. One week later there was a second break-in. I remember there were more polar bear rugs taken but I do not recall how many. Again, Dennis was called down to our office immediately. I followed shortly after. My father was in Yellowknife working with the Inuit for a few weeks and my mother was still working in the office, showing Dennis the ropes. Dennis told the police that the alarm could be disarmed if someone phoned the company number at the same time the building was being entered. Tying up the phone line would block and cancel the alarm.

The police in attendance assumed, wrongly of course, that because Dennis had figured out how to cancel the system and break into the building, he must be the guilty party. In other words, he had executed both robberies. That was absolutely the most ridiculous thing I had ever heard. We were in the process of buying the company from my parents. Since there was no theft insurance, we would be stealing from ourselves. Dennis was promptly taken to the police station for questioning, where he would remain for the next eight hours. He wasn't even allowed one phone call.

In the meantime, my mother and I were questioned extensively. The police were so rude to my mom, treating her as if she was hired cleaning help and not the owner. I was heartsick.

Without any warning they put me in the back of a police car and drove me home, questioning me all the way. They wanted the names of our friends and associates. To my disbelief they searched our home looking everywhere, even under the queen-sized bed which was only raised about eighteen inches from the floor. A polar bear rug with a full head is huge, at least eighteen to twenty-four inches high, and before folding the rugs are anywhere from six to twelve feet long. Try folding fourteen of those and hiding them under the bed! This was such a stupid waste of time. Yes, I know they were just doing their job. My entire life I have had the utmost respect for law enforcement, but why did I keep running into the ones who were clueless?

Dennis was released from police custody. It would take years and years to learn that both robberies were perpetrated by former staff. But there would be more pressing repercussions.

The night before the second robbery Dennis and I were at our local municipal hall for a meeting. We were seeking information on adoption. Although I was only twenty-three years old, my doctor expressed concern that I would not be able to have children. We were prepared to adopt if that was necessary.

Forty-eight hours after the second break-in and Dennis's eight-hour incarceration, I began to hemorrhage. I knew that something was wrong and went to the doctor immediately. I was pregnant. This was a miracle, but I was in the process of a possible miscarriage and I was sent home with strict orders for total bed rest. I spent the next two months flat on my back fighting to save the life of my son. I have always blamed the shock of what happened and the treatment by the police. What they put us through caused this crisis. Our son was born on July 4, 1974, however, and I thank God every day for giving him life. I do not know what I would have done if I had lost my baby.

Now, twenty-two years later I was being questioned by police who again were making a mistake. Soon, I was called into the ER and to Dennis's bedside. There were several doctors and nurses, and we were all surrounded by a curtain. All I remember Dennis saying was, "I've been using cocaine and it will never happen again."

There you have it, a confession. It's done. It's over. A simple misunderstanding has now been cleared up. This nightmare will now come to an end. I had someplace else to be and I had to get back to my perfect life. Dennis would be released in the morning. He had a minor concussion. He looked terrible. That's when I learned he had suffered a cocaine seizure. I left the hospital, put on my happy face, and I drove off. I didn't need to tell anyone about this. I would just say that he slipped in the bathtub and hit his head. We would move forward from here. In that moment of denial, I stepped away from my perfect life and into someone else's shoes. I didn't know that I had just made the single biggest mistake of my life.

Secrets can kill you.

## 3 – All in the Family

I'm afraid of fish. Not saltwater species, not sharks, or even the movie *Jaws*. I'm afraid of freshwater fish like northern pike and trout, and I've been afraid since I was a child. I used to have nightmares about fish eating my pink fuzzy slippers, then my toes, then my feet. When I was a teenager, I spent every weekend on water skis at our summer cottage. If I fell in the middle of the lake and had to wait for the boat to come around, I'd make sure my feet were above water so fish couldn't get them. My fear was even worse if the sun wasn't shining and the water looked dark and ominous.

It would take me over forty years to figure out my fear of fish. A memory came back to me which made it all very clear to me. I was about two years old and my dad traced my foot on a piece of brown paper. I remember standing there in the kitchen while he did it. Then he carved the shape of my foot out of a piece of wood, and put one of my socks on it, followed by one of my white boots. To finish his project, he took the bottom part of a pant leg from a pair of my pants (yellow and green plaid) and wrapped that around the fake foot.

As that very little girl, every time I went to "the shop" to visit my dad and my grandpa at work, the first thing I would see over the door was the last morsel of my leg in the mouth of a northern pike or jackfish. One more swallow and I'd be gone.

The family taxidermy business was started by my grandfather in 1909, beginning where he was born, in Barnsville, Minnesota, and known as J.P. Hawkins Taxidermist. He continued following a move to Canada and the town of Foam Lake, Saskatchewan, where my dad grew up. Our first storefront opened in September of 1949 in Winnipeg's north end. When my father got involved in the business the company name transitioned to J.P. Hawkins & Son. My parents didn't think they could have children, but nine months after they opened the storefront business on Main Street, I was born. When my grandfather died in 1961 my parents bought the business and changed the name again.

Our family business had quite a Royal connection, when the Boy Scouts and Girl Guides sent baby polar bear rugs to Prince Charles and Princess Anne. A photo was published in the local newspaper in August of 1954, which showed my dad putting the final touches on these trophies. This certainly wouldn't be politically correct today.

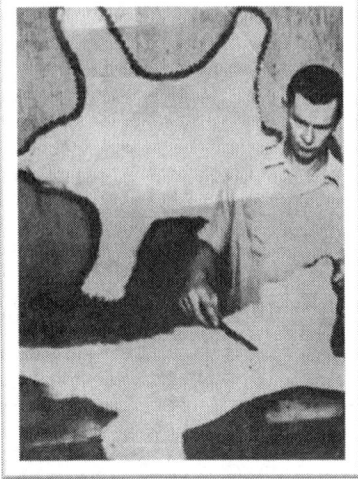

The Hudson's Bay Charter of May 2, 1670 proclaims that when Royalty visits Canada they are to receive two Royal elk heads and a specific number of beaver pelts. When Her Majesty Queen Elizabeth came to Canada in 1959 our company was asked to provide them. This is no longer the practice. In 1967 when Prince Philip, the Duke of Edinburgh opened the Pan American Games in Winnipeg he was given a polar bear rug we mounted. During the duke's visit my parents were even invited to a formal reception. My mother was extremely beautiful, petite, always sun-tanned, with dark hair and big blue eyes. As Prince Phillip walked past them, the prince saw my mom and did a real double-take. My dad always bragged about that event, for he couldn't believe my mom had caught the attention of a prince. In 1971 when Her Royal Highness Princess Margaret, Countess of Snowdon opened the Winnipeg Art Gallery she was presented with one of our full head polar bear rugs.

Also, when Prime Minister Pierre Trudeau made his first visit to China, Chairman Mao was presented with a gift from the Canadian people—another polar bear rug from the Canadian Arctic and mounted by our firm.

We have done work all over the world, but most of our customers were American hunters and fishermen. We had a home taxidermy video course, and we manufactured and stocked all of the components for those who did taxidermy as a hobby.

My mother worked at the shop and ran the office. In the earliest days my grandmother would wash the aprons of the staff weekly. When I was in elementary school my dad would hire me on Saturdays to count and package small components. He would pay me ten cents for my hard work. Even our dog went to the shop every day. It was truly a family business.

# 4 – Finding a Solution

My father was illiterate. Although his siblings received an education, my dad never learned to read or write. He was talented enough to build a successful business, but my mother had to become his eyes and ears. He became very dependent on her for communication and finances and thus very controlling. Dad couldn't have run a business without her.

My dad was very handsome and charming, and to compensate for his lack of education he became a great storyteller. There were two stories my dad told over and over that always made me laugh. They both happened in the '60s when I was a teenager. A local farmer had a cow that gave birth to a two-headed calf. The calf died shortly after birth and the farmer wanted to donate it to a museum, so we were asked to mount it. Once mounted it was displayed in our showroom window for all to see, before the farmer came to collect it. A few months later a guy walked into the building and asked to speak with my dad. Apparently, this man had walked past our building late on a Saturday night after spending too much time at the bar. He was quite drunk when he suddenly saw a small cow with two heads. He knew in that moment he had gone too far and was in serious trouble, so he quit drinking immediately. Now sober for several weeks, he came in to thank my dad for helping him give up alcohol and for saving his life.

In my dad's second tale, two little girls about five and seven were walking past the showroom window when they stopped to press their faces against the screen door to take a look inside. My dad was behind a partition and could see them but couldn't be seen. The older of the two girls said that they killed animals in there to hang on the wall. With that my dad let out a blood-curdling squeal and the oldest said, "Did you hear that, they just killed another one."

I grew up an only child. Both my parents worked in our family business and it had priority over everything else in our lives. When I was nineteen years old my mom and dad wanted to retire, and the advice they were given was to find a son-in-law. I remember that just before I left for a Hawaiian vacation my parents had an appointment with their accountant and lawyer. Selling the business wasn't an easy option. Finding someone to take it over and keep it in the family was. Finding a son-in-law was the perfect solution, and I came to the rescue because I always did as I was told.

I met Dennis within weeks of my parents having this conversation with their accountant. We met the same night I returned from that trip to Hawaii, Saturday, May 2, 1970. It was a really big night in my life. I had cut my vacation short so I could attend a party. It wasn't just any party—it was the party of the century. I worked for the Hudson's Bay Company, and it was celebrating its three hundredth birthday. A history making event! As an employee I had been invited to help make a movie, six months previously, to celebrate and announce all the wonderful things to come for the three hundredth year. It was a fabulous evening of wardrobe choices, hair and makeup sessions as well as the actual filming. We created a party scene that was like a disco setting and we had to film everything twice. The first take was done in English, then we repeated everything with commentary in French.

Finally, May 2 arrived. I had been flying all night from Honolulu, so I was faced with a bit of jet lag. The event was held in the Winnipeg Auditorium, located on the street behind the Hudson's Bay Company parkade. A lot of people were in period costumes, 300 years' worth. When I saw Dennis there, he wasn't a stranger to me. The first time I saw him, the previous November, I knew he was the one. I just knew! He was the most handsome man I had ever seen—very classy looking. I had been following him around the store for the last six months. I remember just before Christmas, Mrs. Wright, our cashier, sent me to the men's suit department to get change. That's when he caught my eye. I came back to our department and said, "Mrs. Wright, I think I have just seen Mr. Right!" Then, the week I was leaving for Hawaii, we sat on the same couch only inches apart in the staff lounge. When he didn't even look my way, I felt defeated and figured that he must be married.

Now only two weeks later, there he was at the party. He was drunk but I think everyone was. I had the cutest hot pink mini dress on, but my feet were killing me from dancing, so I took my shoes off. I overheard him talking about me. I was barefoot and he made some snide comment about my feet matching the rest of me, as I had a Hawaiian tan. My friend Ian told me his name was Dennis, a name I really didn't like. Dennis the Menace, I thought! How right I was. Even though I was there with a date, Dennis asked me out. We had our first date the very next evening.

He pulled up in front of my house in an avocado green 1968 Pontiac Firebird. He was wearing a tweed sports jacket, the kind with the leather patches at the elbow. Oh my God, he was so classy!

I was turning twenty and I'd never had a steady boyfriend. Going to an all-girls school didn't help. Dennis was several years older than me, we were not the same religion, and he had a history. I'd had dates but not that many. Dennis would be my first long-term relationship and he was very easy to fall in love with. I wasn't going to blow it now. Since the age of ten all I wanted was to become a stewardess when I grew up. I couldn't even count how many applications from Air Canada arrived in the mail, but I never filled one out and sent it in. Since I never had a boyfriend, I was afraid I might not be pretty enough or smart enough for the job. Being unattached throughout my teens had left me with an incredible inferiority complex. Now that I'd met someone, I wasn't willing to risk losing him by being relocated to another city for the airline.

My parents were wonderful and understanding about our dating and never interfered. They knew I was head over heels right from the start. They only wanted what was best for me and warmly encouraged our relationship. My parents also wanted someone to take over the family business so they could retire. Dennis was the first candidate and a perfect choice, so they weren't about to protest. I knew all of that and worried that if I let him go no one else would show up to save the business. Love is blind—and it's also color blind to red flags.

Dennis began to work for my parents in our family business one year after we met and six months before our wedding. It was not a good time. His father, George, was terminally ill. Dennis was living at home with his parents, in the midst of his father's battle with cancer. My parents were not the easiest people to work for and he knew nothing about the industry. It was bad but it was just the beginning of really, really bad.

We got engaged on Tuesday, January 19,1971 on the steps of the old auditorium where we had met. The first person I told, even before telling my parents, was Mrs. Wright, the cashier, who, by sending me to get some change, had changed my life. We shed tears of joy together.

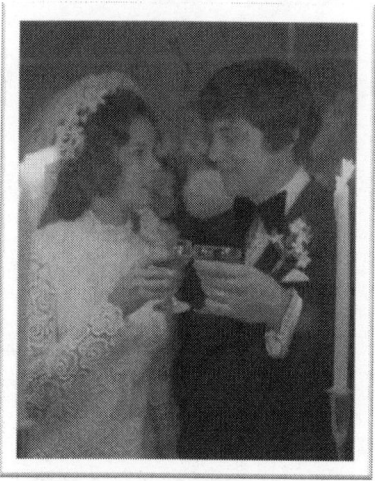

Between July and November of 1971, Dennis and I attended eleven weddings and had been in two wedding parties each. To add to the pressure, I had eleven bridal showers and a trousseau tea. Dennis had a stag party, and our friends threw us a typical Winnipeg social. It's a wonder we made it down the aisle on November 5. In fact, I remember very little of our wedding day. We got married during a huge snowstorm and couldn't leave town the next day for our honeymoon because all the highways were closed.

There is one funny thing that I remember from our wedding. In those days a bride changed from her gown into her "going away" outfit. Mine was a beautiful pink dress topped off with a fitted pink and burgundy plaid winter coat which I purchased at Holt Renfrew. I was very self-conscious that I was a new bride as we checked into our wedding-night hotel. So as not to be conspicuous I stuffed my corsage into my pocket. Of course, I didn't realize that the back of my coat was covered in confetti. We rode silently up the elevator to our room with two other gentlemen. When we stopped at their floor, one man held the door and turned and looked at Dennis. With a wink and a thick Scottish accent, he said, "I know one thing for sure. You'll wake up happier in the morning than me."

Our wedding was the last time his dad was out of the house. My mom always said she thought my father-in-law would have a heart attack in the receiving line. He was so excited to see all of his friends and family in one place. Four weeks later to the day, he passed away. He had been employed with the same company for almost forty years, but because he passed one day before his sixty-fifth birthday, they canceled his pension. That was a terrible thing to have happened to my dear mother-in-law, who really needed that pension. Thirty years later, I would be saying history repeats itself, and lightning strikes twice.

## 5 – Right Under My Nose

After learning that Dennis was addicted to cocaine, he was released from the hospital the next morning. The hospital gave us nothing. Not a phone number, brochure or pamphlet. Not the name of a doctor or support group. It was as if they said, "Don't come back." We had cocaine—snow, crack, flake, blow, white lady, whatever they call it—in our lives and we had nowhere to go. I thought the hospital would help us, perhaps offering solutions like treatment or counseling. Nothing.

Deep down I knew drugs cost a lot of money, but I didn't ask. Nor did I ask where the drugs came from. I didn't want to hear that, because as far as I was concerned it was now in the past. Ignorance is bliss. I was completely unaware that I was so deep in denial I was drowning.

I took Dennis home. I was completely unprepared, naive and ignorant as to the level of despair one would have to be in to become an addict. He said he would stop, and I believed him because there was one thing I knew for sure: our twenty-five-year marriage was based on trust and truth. See what I mean about naive?

Addiction is the result of unresolved grief. If pain never gets healed, it causes more pain. Everything we do in life has an outcome, a consequence. But we aren't programmed to think ahead. Decisions in Dennis's life had been made before my time. No one thought ahead. No one thought of the consequences in the lives around them. It was a done deal, and that deal changed the course of everyone it touched. The ripple effect kept going, kept building for almost thirty years, and now we were being hit by a tsunami.

I thought we had dodged a bullet and life would return to normal. I now realize there is no "normal" when you are living with an addict. I hid from myself, our children and the world. Besides, I had to get back to work. I had a fashion show to plan, to begin a new fashion season, my first as a manager. My business was growing in leaps and bounds.

Business is a great place to hide—but you can only hide for so long before the veneer cracks.

They say that hindsight is 20/20, and after closely examining the time periods just before we learned of Dennis's addiction, yes there were signs that something was wrong. Something was wrong from the very beginning of our relationship and our marriage. But I would never in a million years have believed that whatever was going on with Dennis would lead him to drug use.

Dennis would be the last person on this earth you would suspect of using any kind of drug. We never used drugs ourselves or had them in our home. I do recall, however, in the early '80s, having a client and his much younger girlfriend over for dinner. This young woman asked if "we minded" and pointed to something contained in a small plastic bag. I remember being absolutely horrified, and later Dennis said it was her problem and not ours to judge. They were never invited back.

In October of 1993 the actor and child star River Phoenix died of a drug overdose. At the time, our son, Damien, was living away from home and attending the University of North Dakota. Coincidently Damien bore a strong resemblance to the young actor. I will never forget how upset Dennis was and how worried he was about Damien and drugs on campus.

The very next day he insisted that we pay Damien a surprise visit to once again warn him about the evils and temptations of drugs. We left the following morning and made the two-and-a-half-hour drive across the border. We picked up our son and took him back to our hotel. I went shopping while father and son had a heart-to-heart talk. How ironic and unimaginable that in less than a year Dennis himself would be heavily addicted to cocaine, not snorting the drug as one might suspect, but injecting himself using syringes that we sold in our own taxidermy supply catalogue.

My daughter was just eighteen years old when we discovered, or rather had proof that her dad had a drug problem. Keele is now in her forties, married with three young children of her own. We recently had a conversation during which we recalled the early signs we both saw but ignored.

In the fall of 1994, I found a used syringe on the floor of our family room. In shock I scooped it up. Our daughter was still living at home, and her bedroom, along with her brother's, was just steps away from where the used needle was found. I immediately went to Dennis, who had a logical explanation and put my mind to rest. We had a huge yard. To the north was a narrow park which gave access to the riverbank at the end of our property and could never be claimed as our property. We often saw kids hanging out on the riverbank or in the park itself. There was nothing we could do about it. Except sometimes Dennis would sneak down to our storage area to turn on the underground sprinklers and shower the innocent. That was the only way we could think of to keep trespassers off our property. The sprinkler water was actually river water which was polluted. Dennis thought it was a great joke. On this particular day Dennis claimed that he had found syringes on the riverbank before but did not tell me because it would have upset me. Why would I doubt him?

A month or so later we were at the home of good friends for a dinner party. In casual conversation I brought up the fact that Dennis had found drug paraphernalia in our yard. How I wish the ride home that night had been a short one. Dennis rarely raised his voice to me but that evening he yelled and screamed at me all the way home. His ridiculous reason was that our friends had friends who someday might be interested in purchasing our home and now it had been devalued because they would think there was a drug problem in the area, and it was all my fault. That was crazy. Dennis was talking nonsense. We all lived in high-end homes on pasture-like green yards. No neighbor had ever mentioned a problem and I had never seen gangs or bikers of any sort and it was just neighborhood kids in the area. I now know that Dennis was desperately trying to turn any suspicion away from him and to make sure that I never brought up the subject again.

Just after Christmas, Keele was invited to travel to St. Louis for New Year's Eve. She needed a suitcase but not a large one as she would be gone only a few days. Her dad had a perfectly sized Eddie Bauer bag that he kept under the bed in the guest room, so I mistakenly took it without asking. Dennis had a fit! Then when someone stole the bag from her in St. Louis Dennis completely lost it. He said there was

$1600 US inside one of the side compartments, but I wonder... That was in December of 1994. Were there drugs in there as well? Airport security wasn't as tight as it is now.

Then in January of 1995, about six weeks before Dennis's collapse, I traveled to Toronto for management training followed by a few days in San Antonio. A good friend traveled with me and stayed at our home the night before our flight. It would be over a year later that I finally confessed to her that I was barely coping with my stress and told her that Dennis had a drug problem. Though she had never mentioned it and promised that she told no one except her husband, she too found syringes in our home—in our master bathroom, of all places. Since the guest shower was in the lower level, I had suggested that she use our shower, and it was there, under the carefully folded bath towels, that she found many needles. I too showered in that room but never saw a thing. Keele later told me that while I was away, Dennis spent a very long time, almost daily, locked in the bathroom.

The week before Dennis collapsed, I traveled to Toronto for our annual conference. I took him with me so that he could experience my shining moment. We left our daughter Keele home alone. Weeks later Keele would tell me that for the second time in a few short months she found used needles in the house when no one was there. She knew help was needed for someone, so she took the empty syringes to the RCMP to get answers. There were none. No one would help her, so she kept quiet when we returned.

At the same time Keele had been babysitting three small children who were in our family. She loved them dearly but suddenly without explanation she was dropped. They never called her to babysit again and it broke her heart. It wasn't until 2003 that I learned from another relative that the children also discovered needles in our house and went home and told their mother. Keele never heard from them again.

How blind was I? There was no money missing. Dennis wasn't acting any stranger than usual. But there it was, all of that and more was going on right under my nose.

## 6 – Nothing Changes if Nothing Changes

The weekend of February 24–26, one week after Dennis fell on his head, we both traveled to Calgary and then on to the Kananaskis Resort. It was winter in the Canadian Rockies so we knew it would be a chilly weekend.

We were traveling in a group with my fashion company and this would be my first travel reward. It was also the first time anyone was going to meet my husband. We agreed on the excuse that he had slipped in the bathtub and banged his head so hard that he had a mild concussion. Some of that was true. We couldn't hide the fact that the once black forehead and eye were now a lovely shade of green.

My adrenaline was still pumping. This was a big weekend for me, one I had worked very hard for, and I really didn't know how to act. Dennis was reluctant to take part. That was a common pattern in our marriage. He was a man who stood on the edge, never fully taking part in events, and life in general. This weekend would be no exception. He stood on the sidelines while everyone played broomball, and when we all went dogsledding, I waved goodbye because he wouldn't go. He was polite but wanted to spend more time in our room. Of course, I never thought that he stayed behind to do drugs because he had promised that he would stop, and I had no reason not to believe him.

When we arrived back home it was life as usual, back to normal. What is normal, when your husband is a cocaine addict? He'd had one small slip-up and got caught. He said he would never do it again. Why drag it out? Pretend it never happened and get back to work. Keep pushing and life will move forward. That is just what I did, until Saturday, April 8.

April 8 was my Aunt Gladys's birthday and the family all gathered at her home for dinner to celebrate. Dennis had gone to work that Saturday morning and I hadn't talked to him, but he knew where he had to be at 5 p.m. I had tried to call him, several times in fact, but he never answered, and he wasn't home by noon. Not to worry. I took my own car, and he arrived the same time I did. Of course, he had a full explanation. He had met with an out-of-town client and they went to a restaurant for lunch. His cell phone had died, and the spare battery was in the car. Completely reasonable. He did seem a bit strange, as if he was really wired, and his eyes were as big as saucers. But again, he had a perfect explanation. "My body cannot handle caffeine," he said, adding that he'd had way too much coffee that day. I wasn't even slightly suspicious. It never occurred to me that Dennis was lying to me, but I would soon be confronted with the fact that the lies never stopped.

It was spring, and spring meant Dennis traveled a lot. Six weeks on the road, starting the second week of May. I never questioned him. My birthday came and went the second week of June. I was away and celebrated in Whistler. We had a manager's meeting, and although I was very busy, I could feel stress throughout my body. When our meetings ended, I had a massage to help me relax. I phoned home when I was finished. Dennis never gave me one minute of worry. Drugs were a thing of the past.

I now shudder at my naivety. I was so clueless! Then on Sunday the twenty-seventh of June I could no longer turn a blind eye. Dennis went missing in the middle of the day and I would finally learn to recognize the smell of cocaine.

## 7 – Archie's Bunker

Archie Bunker is a fictional character from the 1970s American television sitcom *All in the Family*. He could've been described as a "lovable bigot." He was also one of Dennis's favorite characters, because Archie reminded him of his Irish Catholic roots and his aunt and uncle's old-fashioned opinions. Archie said what was on his mind in any situation and it was funny. Dennis too would say situationally funny things and he made me laugh.

For his thirtieth birthday I gave Dennis a large pencil sketch of Archie. One day I was in the mall and came across a display of wonderful original portraits of famous people. Archie Bunker's picture jumped out at me because it was so well done, but there was a catch. All the artists were local prison inmates. The one I bought had been done by an inmate incarcerated for forging cheques. No wonder he was such a good artist. (But not quite good enough, he got caught!). Archie's portrait would hang in our home for years to come.

Our home on the river, purchased in 1985, would have been called a California split, with entrances from the lower level as well as the front of the house. Below the double garage was a storage area the same size as the garage, made of cement without windows and just one door. It could have been a designated bomb shelter but in Winnipeg there was little use for that. We immediately dubbed it "Archie's Bunker."

One Sunday in June, when I was still very much in denial, I couldn't find Dennis anywhere. It was lunchtime and he was nowhere to be found. All our vehicles were accounted for and his cell phone was at the back door. Dennis never went anywhere without his cell phone. Perhaps, I thought, he's simply wandered away to chat with a neighbor. So, I waited. I waited well over an hour, then I started to stew. A thought came to me that he might be down in the bunker, puttering, and couldn't hear me call him. I went to the lower level and tried the door, but it was locked. Then, as I walked away a noise came from inside the bunker. He was in there hiding. Locking himself away from our world to shoot up. My heart sank to the ground and I wanted to vomit. I could no longer pretend my life was perfect. I had been living with an addict and he was actively using. Now he was shooting cocaine in our home and I had proof. A rage shot through my body—a red-hot steaming, screaming rage! I wanted to kick down the door, shoot the locks off with a gun or get an axe and chop my way through. But I didn't. I carefully pulled up a lawn chair and sat down in front of the door and softly began coaxing my husband out of his drug den. It took me hours. I pleaded, I begged, I never stopped, and I never let go.

Finally, he stepped out of the bunker, dazed and wild-eyed. There was little I could say or do, but I could clearly smell something odd that I had never smelt before. It was the undeniable stench of cocaine. I was in trouble; my husband was in trouble. He was truly an addict and couldn't stop. This was the beginning of his guilt and remorse phase. We went for a walk around the block, without speaking, and in the silence, I allowed myself to slip back into denial. I didn't have time for this, I had to get packing and put on my happy face again. It was time for us to head west to celebrate my parent's fiftieth wedding anniversary on June 30. There would be a lot to hide from Mom and Dad.

## 8 – Happy Anniversary

It's a big deal when any marriage makes it to fifty years, and a bit of a surprise that my mom and dad's did. Since I'm an only child, celebrating with them both was important to me and an absolute necessity for my mom.

My parents lived in Kelowna, BC during the summer months and we lived in Winnipeg. We came up with the idea of meeting at the halfway point—the same Kananiskis Resort where Dennis and I had gone in February. It was summer now and the weather would be wonderful. It was also going to be Canada Day on July 1, which would make it even more special.

Dennis and I got to Medicine Hat, Alberta the first day and needed a room for one night. I wasn't feeling well so Dennis got us a lovely room with a really big jacuzzi for me to relax in. He was waiting on me hand and foot and was full of "I'm sorry's." The next day we drove into Calgary. When my parents were married in 1945 my mom carried a gardenia, and I did too when Dennis and I were married in 1971. I ordered one to be picked up the next day before we left for the resort. Dennis had to visit a client and I went on a shopping trip with one of my friends. I was back into denial and thought I had no reason to doubt that Dennis wasn't where he said he was. I honestly couldn't have dealt with any other way of thinking.

Less than two years after Dennis started working for my parents, we both realized that we had made a huge mistake, the biggest one we could have ever made. The fighting between my dad and my husband was legendary. More than once they almost came to blows and I was caught smack dab in the middle. In the end my parents sold everything they owned and headed west to begin their retirement. In reality they had to leave the province before someone got killed. I am not kidding. It was that bad.

For the sake of "family" we pretended that things were fine, and when grandchildren were born, I could never keep my parents from them. But our lives were painful and stress-filled whenever we were together. That weekend in Kananaskis at the end of June 1995 was no different. We were all walking on eggshells.

We arrived at the resort June 29 late in the day, so we got together with my parents for dinner and headed to bed early. The resort was beautiful, and our room was lovely and comfortable. The next day was Mom and Dad's fiftieth anniversary, Friday, June 30. Very early in our courtship Dennis and I had attended my parent's twenty-fifth anniversary. Where did the time go? That date, Friday, June 30, would come around the calendar again in five years and completely change my life forever. I could have never predicted back then where our lives were headed.

We got up on the anniversary morning and went for a long drive. The scenery was beautiful, for there is nothing more majestic than the Canadian Rockies, but the Kananaskis Golf Course had been washed out by rains so my parents couldn't go golfing. This would have been the smallest of problems had my dad discovered that my mom was paying for the weekend. We put all our expenses on our credit card, then she slipped us a cheque.

Mom was thrilled with her gardenia corsage and we had a marvelous dinner to celebrate their anniversary. But when I look back at those pictures we took, I looked very strange. It was as if I had been blown up like a marshmallow. I looked very plump and spongy. We headed to bed fairly early because I didn't feel well. It was terribly hot in our room—so hot that Dennis had to order a fan and fill the garbage can with ice water so I could use a facecloth to sponge myself to cool my body down. I was burning up and felt nauseous, but in the morning I was much better. I thought it was just something I ate. It was July 1, Canada Day. There were celebrations at the resort and then we drove into Banff for dinner to continue the party. Everything about the weekend went off without a hitch. No small miracle.

# 9 – Too Hot to Handle

We returned home from my parent's anniversary weekend and I was still unprepared to do anything about Dennis's drug problem because I didn't have a clue what to do. I didn't know why I was so paralyzed. Looking back, it was more about embarrassment than anything else. I was still horrified that my husband was a drug addict, and I did not want anyone to know. In fact, it was a very long time before I shared my pain with anyone. I didn't even tell our children. As far as they knew, their dad had quit when he said he would. This theme would keep reappearing, I just couldn't talk about it.

About a week after we came home, Dennis and I were off to the Winnipeg Stadium to see a football game. I'm a huge football fan and we had season tickets since 1985. Most games my son went with me. It became our thing. Dennis rarely went. This particular game was the first of the season and the first game in our new seats, which were in the upper deck. That meant a long walk up a curved ramp. Not difficult normally, but by the time we got to our seats I was having difficulty breathing. I felt worse by the minute, so after the first half of the game we headed home. Much later that night we were expecting friends from Toronto who would be staying with us while attending a wedding. I spent the entire weekend in bed and saw very little of our company. I was leveled by another fever that reached 104 °F, for the second time in just two weeks. It was now time to see a doctor and find out what was wrong.

When we had been in Calgary in June, Dennis visited a client who had just returned to Canada from Africa and came back quite sick. When we started the search to find out what was wrong with me, Dennis even phoned the client, thinking that maybe he had passed on whatever disease he had to Dennis and then on to me. The timing was right. But the timing was also right about my fevers and Dennis's drug use, so in my heart I felt it was all connected. Nothing showed up in my blood work, so I pulled some strings with a friend who got me in to see the head of Infectious Diseases at one of the city's largest hospitals. This doctor turned me inside out for months, with blood work, CT scans, X-rays and weekly visits. We ruled out Lyme disease, but all he found was a chronic sinus infection, which would not cause such debilitating fevers, and nothing else.

The scenario was always the same. I would start seeing flashing white lights in front of my eyes, which I called sparklers. They would be followed by extreme chills. I could barely stand up when this happened. I would have to go right to bed. If I was somewhere else when it started, I went straight home and into bed because I would shake uncontrollably. I would pack my bed with heating pads, hot water bottles and heated bean bags. Anything to get me warm. Then the fever itself would set in and last approximately twelve hours, during which time I would sweat so much that using every single towel in the house under me wasn't enough. And I would cough, cough and cough! The amount of sweat that poured out of me could have floated a boat, but no doctor advised me as to how to deal with these fevers. I knew nothing about electrolytes and dehydration. I never ate much during these episodes and sipped on fruit juices, which were full of sugar, instead of drinking water.

I would be flat on my back for days at a time. Two dogs at my feet and two phone lines. That's how I built my business. When I felt well enough, I made calls and my business kept growing. I often went out for work with my high fevers and Dennis would drive me and pick me up.

Dennis continued doing drugs and I continued not to ask questions. He always had this "thing" about his cell phone. When it rang, he always answered it immediately. If he got a message, he would return the call right away. That was business. But in the fall of 1995 his phone went unanswered for hours and hours several times a week. I can remember doing training with my team at my home, usually on a Saturday morning. and at every break I would call Dennis—not to talk to him but just to find him. If he didn't answer, I had a term for his absence. He had gone to "skid row," because that is how I felt and how I dealt with it. Whatever he did or didn't do, one of my fevers would inevitably follow.

## 10 – Skid Row

I was still so horrified that my husband was an addict that I told no one or any of the doctors I was seeing. As part of the description of what my fevers entailed, I would always say that I was living with tremendous amounts of stress, but no physician asked, "what kind of stress?"

It wasn't stress. I was living in terror. There is no other way to describe it. I never knew what was coming next. In the fall of '95 I was in bed sick and sobbing when a good friend phoned. She knew something was wrong and had been for a long time, and she begged me to tell her. I finally gave in and asked her to come right over. There, while still in bed I told her what I had been living with for six months, and suddenly she collapsed on my bedroom floor and burst into tears. As a result, I was the one comforting her the rest of the afternoon. No one would ever believe that Dennis was a druggie. He was everyone's hero. I swore her to silence and made the decision that I would never tell anyone else.

From the fall of 1995 to summer of 1996, I experienced situations no wife should ever have to endure.

In October my computer wasn't working, and I needed to write a newsletter, so I decided to go to the shop and use one in the office. Our office manager said that Dennis had gone out for lunch and should be back soon. I sat and typed and typed some more. Time passed and Dennis had not returned so I tried phoning him, but he didn't answer. Remember, answering the cell phone was a huge issue: he never liked to miss a call. That is, of course, unless he went to skid row.

More hours passed, then suddenly my stomach sank, and I knew where he was. I slipped back to Dennis's office and very quietly let myself in. I could smell the cocaine in the air. The boardroom door was closed and locked, but I could see a small crack of light at the bottom of the door. My heart sank once again. He was in there. He'd hidden his truck down the street and walked back to the building, snuck in and locked himself in where no one would think to look. He was shooting up. I lay on the floor and begged and cried for him to stop. Through the crack of light on the floor I pleaded with him to come out. Finally, around four thirty, after two hours of begging, he did emerge, dazed and wild-eyed, and I had to drive him home. He was incapable of getting behind the wheel. We never spoke of the incident again.

One night a few weeks later, he failed to show up after work. Sometime after midnight I went out to search for him. I went into our building. It was almost 17,000 square feet and he could be anywhere in there. Maybe he wasn't there, maybe he was. I never knew. I searched all three floors, the washrooms and every corner of the building. I was shaking in my boots. Halfway through the warehouse there was a furnace room. I have no idea why I even thought to look there, because it was a very small room, more like a closet. I opened the door and there he was sitting on a barrel in his underwear, with a belt strapped around his thigh, shooting up. All I remember is the sound of my screams. Blood-curdling, bone-chilling, painful screams. I have no idea what happened next. I've completely blocked it out.

Another night in the dead of winter, I went searching again when he didn't come home. This time I had somehow gotten the name of the place where he bought his drugs, but I didn't even know if this was true. I drove down that street looking for his truck, found the bar and parked my car across the street, and just sat and cried. I looked in my rearview mirror and a police car was parked right behind me. I was terrified! Dennis never came out. The police left, and I still didn't have a clue where he was, so I gave up. On the way home I saw a phone booth at the corner. I pulled in and called the police. I don't think I dialed 911, I simply found a number in the phone book. In total distress I begged whoever was on the other end of the phone to help me. I was absolutely desperate, and I cried and begged some more. Then I hung up, got back in my car and drove myself home. I have no idea when Dennis showed up, and I didn't ask.

Once January came, Dennis had to travel. He was gone more often than he was home, each month to a different city promoting our business. I have no idea how he managed his road trips or if he did drugs on the road. Two more times I went off to rescue him when he was back home. It's no wonder that I was so sick.

It must have been -40 °C one late night when once again Dennis didn't show up for dinner. I instinctively went to our building because I knew he thought no one could find him there, and this time I couldn't. I called out over and over, and searched every inch of the place, almost sick to my stomach. I decided to leave in hopes that maybe he had come back home already. As I walked past the ladies' washroom, the door moved, and I froze on the spot. I then pushed on the door and Dennis was inside. Once again, I was in a situation no wife should find herself in with her husband. I screamed and screamed and screamed.

He locked himself in the boardroom another time that spring after his travels were complete. When I found him then something snapped inside of me. I think I had reached my limit. I went out to the shipping department and found a large piece of PVC pipe. Fortunately, there wasn't an axe or a piece of heavy metal. I started screaming and bashing in the door. I needed this! One entire side of the door was damaged, but I couldn't get through to the other side. That was probably a good thing, because I think I just may have killed my husband if I had gotten through that door. My rage was overwhelming. Instead of replacing the door, Dennis taped a large calendar over the damage I created. It stayed like that for many, many years. No one knew what had happened. We'd covered up the evidence. We were very, very good at covering up.

## 11 – The Secret Behind the Secret

I didn't tell anyone that Dennis was an addict. I was too embarrassed; and besides, no one would have believed me. He was truly a wonderful person to all who knew him. What could possibly make a person, any person, desperate enough to turn to drugs? What would possess Dennis to take drugs? A man who was truly successful by all appearances, and who had everything in life one could possibly want. In 1995 when Dennis "fell on his head" I couldn't fathom what the reason could be. I really couldn't.

Dennis rarely if ever talked about his childhood. I really don't think he had one. His family never went anywhere or owned a car and Dennis was very, very overprotected. He wasn't allowed to skate or play hockey because he could get his teeth knocked out or his nose broken. He was never allowed to learn to swim or go to the YMCA because child predators lurked in the change rooms. His parents were a bit older, as his dad was over forty when Dennis was born. I remember when we talked about having children, he said he would never be like his dad—too old, tired and uninterested to play a simple game of catch with his son. His sister Mary-Jane was five years older. They never had much in common as children or as adults.

His parents smoked unfiltered cigarettes. His mother smoked until the day she died. Homes were small then and poorly ventilated. As a child he was often sick with pneumonia. His lungs were scarred, and he missed so much school that he failed one or more grades. Even after we met and married, a simple cold would force him to bed for weeks. He was a candidate for yearly chest X-rays, but you can't make men do something they don't want to do.

Beyond all of this, Dennis had a huge secret, one he had never brought up; and slowly I realized that this secret had been eating him up for twenty-five years. A secret that was never discussed that he had buried long in the past. It became my secret too. I kept quiet as well and pretended that none of it had ever happened.

Back in May of 1970 we had our second date, one week after our first, and that's when he told me his story. At twenty-three, he was going through a divorce. The marriage should have never happened, but they were expecting a child. In 1967 that was referred to as, "They had to get married," because that is just what you did back then. It didn't last long for many reasons, but the big one was religious differences. He was an Irish Catholic, and she was Jewish. They stayed under the same roof almost two years, during which time Dennis said he took almost total care of the baby. From what he told me it was two years of hell. The marriage would be annulled by the Catholic Church, the first marriage annulled by the pope in the history of Manitoba. "The child" —that's how he referred to his son—was now almost three years old and Dennis was forced to give him up.

It was always "the child." Dennis never called him by name. That should have been a clue for me. I can't put enough emphasis on the fact that Dennis told me this was what he wanted. He felt that "the child" was young enough to eventually forget that he even had a dad. He felt it unfair to push and pull a child between parents with weekly custody, sharing holidays and annual vacations. He did a really good job of convincing me that he was right, but I think he was really trying to convince himself. I told him from the beginning that I would happily accept a child of his at any age and time. I now see that was very stupid and naive on my part, as I was totally unequipped. I didn't even see the biggest part to his past because I was not a parent. I had no clue how deep a parent's love goes. It wasn't until our son was born that "I got it," but by then it was too late.

Dennis came from a large and loving extended family, but he felt he had brought shame to the family name by divorcing and giving up his child. He told me that it made him think that all the aunts, uncles and cousins hated him. His family lost not only a daughter-in-law but also a grandson and nephew, someone near and dear to them for his first three years. This was not Dennis's choice. In order to be granted a divorce from his wife the primary condition was there could be no contact with his son for the remainder of his life. I now know that keeping a child from a parent, because you are angry or want to get even, is a form of child abuse. His son was denied a lifetime of love from a wonderful man and a fabulous family.

I remember that shortly after we were married the Oscar-winning movie "Kramer vs. Kramer" was released and it was all the rage that year. Dennis and I had an argument because he wouldn't go to see it. I didn't realize that the story line of the movie closely resembled his, a custody battle and the loss of a child. When Dennis told me his story, after our second date, he had me really convinced that he was in agreement with the conditions that were laid before him. I couldn't see then that his explanation was all a cover-up.

A parent never recovers from the loss of a child, whether it's from a death or divorce. In a parent's heart it's the same thing. Dennis never recovered, never grieved, never dealt with it. But his reaction to the pain and loss affected everyone. If the pain is never healed, it causes more pain. Still the subject was never, ever talked about. In my thirty years being part of his family, I can only remember the subject of his son's disappearance discussed once and then only vaguely. It also took a long time for some in the family's inner circle to trust me when I came into the picture. Dennis had been hurt so deeply that the wound was still fresh, and I had to prove my love and loyalty.

Very few of our friends knew that Dennis was divorced, and even fewer knew that he'd already been a father but didn't have a son. We just never brought up the subject. Even though Dennis swore he would be an active dad unlike his own, when we did have children it was an entirely different story. The fear of losing again never left him, so I always felt that he failed to completely bond with our own children in the way I would have expected. It was as if he was terrified that I would leave and take our children with me.

## 12 – I Have a Secret Too

In early July of 1977 our son turned three years old and our daughter turned one. I had decided, after she was born, that I would not have any more children and would do something about it. We discussed it and decided that Dennis would have a vasectomy; but I wanted to wait until our youngest was a year old because I was, like any young mother, terrified of crib death. So little was known about it back then. Then one day out of the blue Dennis announced that he had changed his mind and his vasectomy had to be done sooner than that, or he wouldn't do it. I was stunned and still wanted to wait, but nothing I said could change his mind. Now that the year was up, something had to be done and it was up to me. If I wanted to prevent a future pregnancy, I would have to have my tubes tied. Because he put work before family, Dennis would never look after our children, and I would have to wait until October, when my mom could come to look after them.

One morning I woke with a terrible, terrible feeling and I just knew I was pregnant for the third time, in spite of using double precautions. Once you've been through two pregnancies you just know that feeling. I could not have another child! It was now six years into our marriage, and we were seeing a psychiatrist for marriage counseling. I made an appointment to see him immediately. Dennis knew I was going, knew my surgery was booked for October and absolutely knew I didn't want another child. I will never, ever forget sitting there sobbing and asking for advice because I really didn't know what to do. This doctor told me he had five wonderful children and if I agreed to see him once a week for the next nine months he would "get me through" another pregnancy. If he thought he was helping me. he really was. In fact, it was the best advice I'd ever been given because in that moment I swore to myself that there was no bloody way a man behind a desk, who knew nothing about me, was going to tell me what to do with my body.

Within a few days I began to hemorrhage. There was no doubt that I would be confined to my bed if I was to keep this pregnancy. I'd been down this road before. Dennis and I discussed this at length, and he told me over and over that it was my decision and that he would support whatever I decided. I wanted to terminate the pregnancy immediately. Over forty years later I sit here and cry as I write this. My mind was made up and it was the most difficult and darkest decision I have ever made. I consulted my family doctor and was given the name of a clinic in Grand Forks, North Dakota. I would have to leave the country to terminate my pregnancy.

On the day we drove south, Dennis took the big economy van that we used for our business. It had the rear bench seat removed and I begged him to put it back in because I knew I would not feel well and would like to be able to lie down on the drive home. He wouldn't do it. We arrived in Grand Forks and found the address. On a day when I needed my husband more than ever, he dropped me at a bus stop, and I walked alone down the street to the clinic. When I was finished, I walked back to the bus stop and waited on the bench until he picked me up. He didn't ask me a single question.

When we returned home, Dennis disappeared, and I was left with a three-year-old and a one-year-old to bathe and put to bed. I was in a great deal of pain, both physically and emotionally. We didn't have air conditioning at that time and the house was stifling so I went in search of my husband to get him to help me with the kids. I found him in the basement on the floor wearing a headset and listening to music while drinking a bottle of Scotch. When I touched him to get his attention, he took off the headset and looked at me with dismay and disgust and said, "Don't you ever touch me again. You are a murderer and you have made me your accomplice!"

Two days later I packed up my children and got on a plane to visit my parents for two weeks. I needed to be safe and to feel unconditional love. It took me years to realize that to Dennis, I was just another woman who took a child from him. We never brought the subject up again, but I have lived with my decision every single day of my life.

## 13 – On My Own

When I did get pregnant the first time in 1974, I spent the first few months flat on my back in bed fighting to save my pregnancy, but there continued to be health concerns. I spent the last month in the hospital on total bed rest. Once our beautiful son was born, Dennis changed. I wasn't allowed to take any pictures of the baby even though I had my camera in my hospital room. Dennis told me the flash would cause baby blindness, and because I'd never had a baby before, I believed him. After all, he had experience.

I couldn't nurse my son and I was terribly upset. On the last Sunday I was in the hospital, Dennis didn't come to visit me. We, or rather he, had put an in-ground swimming pool in our back yard. When I phoned him to come up to visit me, he was having a pool party. In tears I begged him because I was very upset that I couldn't nurse. Dennis told me that if I didn't nurse, I wasn't a "real" woman and he hung up. My night nurse had to bring me a tranquilizer because I was so upset and couldn't be calmed down.

I truly thought that once Dennis had another child, and in particular another son, things would change. Tragically he didn't see what he was about to gain, only what he had already lost. Once I got home it didn't get any better. Dennis wouldn't hold the baby and refused to change, bathe or feed him. I also wasn't allowed to get a change table. His answer to that was, "*She* didn't have a change table, you don't need one either." He set up a small card table for me to use until his mother and mine went behind his back and bought me a proper baby change table. I wasn't allowed to go out at any point until the baby was down for the night.

One evening I went late to my ceramics class and came home to a screaming baby. Dennis was sitting watching TV, tuning out the baby's cries because he refused to change a diaper. I honestly did not equate the loss of his son to the impossible attitude toward his new family. It was never talked about. This was 1974 and I began to feel that the responsibility of both a home and a business he was trying to build, but really knew nothing about, was too much pressure for him to handle. Now with the addition of a son I really felt it was too much stress for him and hoped that, in time, he could relax and enjoy life more.

When our son was eight months old, I ended up in the ER at 6 a.m. with abdominal pain and had to have an emergency appendectomy. Once I was home, Dennis refused to even take an afternoon off to help me. I could not lift a baby, so he brought in his mother to help. She had health problems and couldn't lift a twenty-pound baby either, so I had to do it anyway.

By the time our second child arrived in June of 1976, nothing on the home front had changed. When our daughter was only a few weeks old Dennis left us. I stood in the driveway crying hysterically and pleading with him not to leave. With a newborn in my arms and a two-year-old at my side, I was terrified he wasn't coming back. The birth of a child is supposed to be one of the happiest times in your life. He did return after a week. He said he needed a break.

Don't we all.

Dennis had to travel for business, but most of the time I felt like a single parent. When he was home, I couldn't understand why our friends took holidays with their children and we didn't. Dennis used the business as an excuse, but our friends were entrepreneurs as well and they could find the time. We had a basement full of camping equipment but went on a camping trip only once. That one time we lasted only five hours before we packed up everything and came home. Our very first "family" vacation was Christmas in Florida when our children were eleven and thirteen. It certainly wasn't because we couldn't afford it.

One Christmas I had a professional portrait done of the children and me, not too large but very appropriate for his office and new boardroom. He would never put it on display. I found it at the bottom of a closet. He said it would make him and the company seem like a Mickey Mouse operation. Family photos weren't even allowed in our home, and although my mom gave us one of the first handheld video cameras, I only have one family video, which I had to hide from him.

For our entire marriage Dennis traveled from January to April doing the Sport Show circuit. After the last show of the season Dennis would host a big cocktail party where everyone could unwind after the long winter. Nine months after my abortion, Dennis was traveling to Minneapolis for the last show and I really wanted to go with him. I was still suffering in silence but needed to get away. Dennis agreed that I could come with him, so we flew down. But when I got there, he made me get a separate hotel room and I was not allowed to come to the party. I was absolutely heartbroken and humiliated. Again, he used the excuse that he didn't want to send the message that we were a "mom and pop" company, but it made me feel like there was something wrong with me. His secretary was invited but I wasn't.

A few years later I wanted to take my son with us, as he was old enough to travel. Again, I was relegated to another room in the hotel and was not to be seen. At the beginning of the week, I even had to stay at a different hotel. Another time I took both children for spring break in Minneapolis, but Dennis flew, and I had to make the nine-hour drive with two kids aged seven and nine. We stayed in the same hotel as their dad but nowhere near him.

Another heartbreak came in 1986 when Vancouver hosted Expo 86, the World's Fair. Our company was a corporate sponsor, which gave us free and easy access to any and all pavilions as well as the opening and closing ceremonies. I also worked for an airline and could get us passes for free travel, but Dennis would not go, not even for a few days. I never understood that one.

For two summers, once our children were in their early teens, I rented a cottage with a girlfriend at Victoria Beach, northeast of Winnipeg. We would all drive there in a car loaded to the top. Dennis would just drop us and our belongings off. He wouldn't stay overnight or even stay for lunch like my friend's husband. He was gone just as soon as we were dropped off. I truly felt abandoned and couldn't understand why he didn't want to be with us.

Another time I did buy tickets to see my favorite entertainer, Mac Davis, who was appearing in Jamestown, ND. Our neighbors and good friends also bought tickets and we planned the trip together. We would hire sitters to look after our children and fly down in their private plane. We would have a nice dinner, see the concert, stay overnight and return the next morning. We would only be gone twenty-four hours. But the morning we were to leave, Dennis changed his mind and refused to go. There I was with no husband at my side to enjoy life with me. My heart broke one more time.

Why did I stay with him? Why didn't I just pack up my children and leave? Well, actually I did leave once, and it lasted about an hour and a half. I simply drove around with both kids in the car and thought about what I wanted and where I could go, and I made the decision to go home.

I loved Dennis. I really, truly loved him and together we had taken a vow—"till death do us part." And, when you love someone you do everything to make it work. He was never violent or physically abusive. He was generous to a fault. I had more bouquets of long-stemmed roses than anyone I knew. He never came home from a business trip without some little gift for me, a thank-you for holding down the fort while he was out of town. I remember once he brought me a gardening caddy to hold all my tools. I was a lousy gardener back then, truly clueless, but he gave me those tools to help make me better.

I fondly remember an event that happened on one of our Sunday drives. We were stopped at a red light downtown, in front of a mall. There on the corner sat a young teenage boy who by all appearances was homeless. Dennis and I both turned our heads and noticed him but never said a word. When we got home and pulled into our driveway, Dennis said that he would drop me off and then go back to the shop. I just looked at him and said, "You're going back to help that young boy on the corner, aren't you?" His answer was yes; and I wanted to go along too. Back we went and found a parking spot not far from where we had seen this young man. We were both relieved to see that he was still there, and Dennis offered to buy him lunch. So, we took this young man into the mall and bought him all he could eat and then some so he would have more later. Dennis mentioned to me on the way home that it would kill him to ever think his own children were on the street. That was the other side of Dennis that I knew. He had a tremendously generous soul and never wanted to see anyone suffer.

When we moved into our big house there was a lot of clearing and yard work to be done. Dennis could have easily hired a landscape company. One day the doorbell rang, and it was a very scruffy man looking for any kind of work we could give him. Just behind him was a small boy and a very pregnant woman and they were all on foot. Dennis hired him on the spot, and they were there every day for a week. Dennis admired the fact that they were not only willing to work but did the best job they could. We fed them often and in the end Dennis paid them far more than quoted.

Despite his generous spirit, I realized that I had married a broken man, and I was beginning to understand that Dennis harbored tremendous guilt for not having fought for custody of his son. I could never take our children away from him, for it would have killed him. I would learn later that truly was his greatest fear. In his mind I was building my business so that I would have the cash I needed to start a new life without him.

There was another reason I didn't leave him. If I left with our children, nothing was holding Dennis in Winnipeg. He could have walked away and started a new life in another city or country. He always told me that he wished he'd gone to Australia to start over when his first marriage ended. Now he could leave me with a business that I knew nothing about. A business that employed forty-five people. A business that I was never supposed to be involved in. That would have brought me to my knees. Love is strong but sometimes fear is greater.

Yes, Dennis had many flaws and when I finally realized using drugs was a way of masking his pain, I also knew that he was about to crack. Help and the answers my husband needed were just around the corner.

## 14 – Breaking Point

My fevers continued throughout the winter of 1996 and Dennis was never there for me. If I was sick, he would leave. Even if he was home and not on the road, I would be alone. I would find out several years later that when I got a fever he went to his best friend's house where he would sit and cry, terrified that I was going to die. He just couldn't deal with me being sick. Each time my fever spiked at 104 °F I feared I would have a seizure. I was in my mid-forties and obviously not healthy. The doctors had no answers, so we just kept looking. I kept my neighbor's phone number on speed dial. She was a nurse and although she never knew what was going on inside our home, I felt comforted that I could call on someone. Fortunately, I never had to.

Almost one year to the day after Dennis "fell on his head" I was awakened early one morning. My bed was shaking like there was an earthquake. When I sat upright, I was shocked to see that Dennis was sitting at the end of our bed, head in his hands, and crying as I had never seen him cry, sobbing like a child. I was absolutely stunned, and I asked him what was wrong. All he said was the name of his son, a name I had never heard him use because he always referred to his son as "the child." I knew in my heart that we had found a place to start.

He told me he had been up all night writing a letter to his son, whom I will refer to as John. He needed the letter to be typed, and he handed it to me as he continued to cry. Finally, after all these years, Dennis was opening up. John was the third person in the room for our entire marriage and the missing piece in our family. By reaching out to his son by letter, breaking his promise, he was giving himself permission to finally express his feelings and in turn heal his wounds, after twenty-five years. I knew this man. There was a part of him that was a wonderful caring person, but he had spent twenty-five years living in regret and remorse; and when you hold things in, it can cause a whole lot of physical and emotional damage. I never brought up the subject of John, and I knew this would be the beginning of peeling back those layers of pain. This letter was a start, a place to begin solving the mystery of why Dennis turned to cocaine. It would be a very slow start but at least it was a start.

After I typed the letter, Dennis told me that he had found the address in another city where he thought his son lived. He put the package together and along with the letter he sent two baby pictures, a birth certificate and a copy of the divorce papers. He sent it by bus, and I have no idea why. It was not my place to question. I left the subject open. If Dennis wanted to share his son's response, I knew that he would.

## 15 – One More Time

In April of 1996 we were booked on a Caribbean cruise, a reward through the company I was with, but I was dreading the trip. Again, I was so unsure of Dennis and his drug use and fearful of going through customs in each country where we docked. My stress level was at its maximum. There was no evidence that Dennis was using on the trip, but he kept to himself and away from the group as much as possible. He simply did not want to join in.

In May Dennis started his road trips again and things seemed to be going fine. I required surgery in early June and my mom came to visit and help me out. When she left, things went downhill very fast. One day I couldn't find Dennis and went to our building. I went to the boardroom to search for him, but he wasn't there. Suddenly something possessed me to look under the cushions of the couch, and to my absolute horror there must have been two hundred used syringes. I went home and waited. Late into the evening there was still no Dennis and I was at my breaking point. I phoned his best friend, Ron, and asked him to come over. I had to tell someone. When I told Ron, he called me a liar—even after I showed him the plastic garbage bag full of used syringes that I had brought home from Dennis's office. I begged Ron to come to the shop again with me. I was so fearful that one of these times I would find a body. We searched the building but no Dennis. He showed up the next day apparently after driving east just to escape.

This was showdown time.

I gave Dennis an ultimatum. He had to get help or else. It took a few days, and I couldn't be involved in his decision because if he wanted help, he had to do this for himself. I don't know where he got the information, but he decided to go to St. Joseph's Hospital in Thunder Bay, Ontario, and that's when then things got really weird.

About a week before, I'd come home to find the garage door open, and the clothes Dennis had been wearing were strewn all over the garage floor. I followed the path of clothing down the hall to our bedroom. Because we had had a terrible windstorm the night before, he had pulled out the ladder to check the roof but did not set it up properly, and it fell with him on it. Dennis was lying on the bed in great pain. His left shoulder was broken, and it was off to the ER again. His mind just wasn't working right, either. He decided that if he was going into drug treatment for four to six weeks, he needed to come up with an excuse for not being around the office. A broken shoulder was a perfect reason not to be at work, but he would create another story instead. He would tell everyone he was going to Russia on a fishing trip. Unbelievable! I told him that he couldn't do that. Friends would want to see pictures and hear stories—and how was he going to travel and fish with a broken shoulder?

For addicts, deceit and lies become a way of life. Every day brought a new and bigger lie.

Dennis left for Thunder Bay and treatment in early July. He felt that the long trip, driving at least eight hours both ways, was too strenuous for my health, so our son Damien drove his dad. Apparently soon after they arrived, one of the hospital staff turned to Damien and said, "You can put your bags in this room." Damien turned to him and said, "It's not for me, it's for my dad." No child ever should be put in that position.

One of the rules for drug treatment was no contact with the outside world, so I didn't have a choice. I couldn't phone or write. I started seeing a naturopath, still in search of what was causing my fevers. I tried supplements and diets—whatever someone suggested, I tried. That summer was very healing for me, physically and emotionally. Just the weight of not having Dennis around to make me worry made me feel better. The worry wasn't there while he was out of sight.

September came and Dennis was home, and life for the first time in eons seemed normal. I still had my fevers, but they were predictable, and I wasn't dead yet. I was now in search of an explanation at another Winnipeg Hospital. I seemed to be passed from one department to another, but each new doctor was as baffled as the rest. I put my nose to the grindstone and kept building my business in spite of spending ten days a month flat on my back in bed.

One evening Dennis said he would be home later than me. He had been out of treatment a month and I was not expecting him ever to slip back into his old ways. I decided to finish up my work and dropped by the office to see him. When I looked at him, I knew instantly that he had been doing drugs. He was high on cocaine—his eyes were wild, and I could smell it in the air. He had no time to lie or explain. I collapsed and dropped to the ground in some sort of seizure and lost all bladder control. I remember nothing. But I think that was the moment Dennis finally realized he was responsible for whatever this was, and he was killing me.

## 16 – Parent Trap

From the moment the ink was dry on our marriage certificate my parents and my husband were at war. As an only child, my husband's relationship with my parents was extremely important to me. I wanted everyone to get along. I dreamed of weekends at their cottage and big trips together. But by the time Dennis and I were in the process of purchasing the business which included the building, things were on very thin ice. With all the anger and frustration between them I was very afraid that Dennis and my dad would come to blows.

In the fall of 1975, my parents sold their home and set out for British Columbia and retirement. They would spend their summers in the Okanagan area, and they would become snowbirds in the winter. They started with a camper and a truck and went in search of a place to purchase a home in Arizona. The decision for them to move away from us and the business was made so that we could save our marriage. Dad and Dennis could not be in the same city; and if they were living in different provinces at least Dad wouldn't be on our doorstep. I mean my dad would come to our apartment and bang on the door to try and get our attention. On many occasions I hid in the bathroom and pretended no one was home. However, for the next twenty-four years, good ole Dad did everything possible to destroy my husband in business.

Many, many friends warned us not to take over my parents' company; and how I wish we had listened. At one point in late 1975 Dennis was offered a great job in Edmonton. We could have changed our minds about taking over the family business and started fresh in another city, but Dennis wouldn't. He simply didn't want to look bad, like a quitter, and he insisted on keeping the deal going. This was his own lack of confidence and self-esteem. If he was successful in business, he felt he would be redeemed by his own family, and so keeping our family business growing was a huge motivation.

Big mistake.

The downhill slide started when we were on our honeymoon in November of 1971, a week after we were married. We called home to check in and my dad insisted we return home immediately. Things were too busy, he said, for Dennis to take any time off. It was our honeymoon. Three weeks later, my new father-in-law died of cancer and even though Dennis had talked to both my parents over the weekend, my dad never got over the fact that Dennis didn't phone him on Monday and ask for time off.

Once we purchased the company and they were gone, both Mom and Dad acted as if they had never left. My parents were out and were paid handsomely each month. They had their freedom but felt free to criticize our every move. When they came to town for a visit they would walk in as if they still owned the place. My mom would say she just wanted to talk to the girls in the office, then she would start rifling through files. And Dad would go upstairs to shoot the breeze with the staff on our dime. He would also help himself to whatever he wanted in the building. One time while we were away on a trip both my parents came to look after the children—I hated to deny them access to their only grandchildren. Our guest room had a large closet but in it was a double-size mattress that we were storing. It ticked Dad off that he had limited space to hang his clothes, so once we left, he drove a spike into the bedroom wall big enough to hold ten hangers! He also put a nail in the front of the bar cupboard so that he could hang up his bottle opener. I honestly thought Dennis would kill him.

The real damage came in 1981 when the Canadian postal service was on strike. Between 1974 and 1981 there were four postal strikes and two were over six weeks long. At that time every penny came to us via mail, with personal cheques or money orders. No one used credit cards back then. Since we had been faced with postal strikes three times already, Dennis asked my dad if he could defer our monthly payments to him until the strike was over. We had just added a warehouse on to the existing building. We needed to pay staff, pay our bills and feed our children. My dad agreed to the terms, then called our bank manager, who was a personal friend of his, to let the bank know that we weren't making our monthly commitment. My dad also took me aside and showed me his rudimentary bookkeeping so that I would understand he was losing money. It was all about his 16 percent interest, the going rate back then. My husband lost fifty pounds in two months from the stress.

The word *spite* is defined as "a desire to hurt, annoy, or offend someone," and Dennis's relationship with my dad was solidly built on spite. Dennis was not a hunter or fisherman, but he became exposed to that lifestyle once he met me. He bought his first shotgun and then he bought a second. My dad said, "Why would you buy a second gun when you can only shoot one at a time?" That was all the motivation he needed. Dennis said nothing but over time bought more than a hundred shotguns.

Once my parents moved away, Dennis bought three new vehicles: an economy van for the business, a wood-paneled station wagon for our family, and a beautiful bronze Oldsmobile Cutlass with swivel front seats for me. We paid cash, we were never in debt and never had a home mortgage, but if you heard my dad's complaints you would think Dennis was spending beyond our means and bleeding him dry.

In twenty years, we only visited my parents twice as a family. A marriage counselor gave Dennis a warning that he couldn't keep me from my parents and shouldn't make me choose between them. When Mom and Dad did come to town, I spent my time walking on eggshells. Dennis would stay out very late, almost every night, doing I don't know what. He just didn't want to be around because the stress between my parents and him was so thick you could cut it with a knife.

Today I have very little to remind me of my parents. For some strange reason whatever gifts they gave me or us would disappear over time. Dennis wanted nothing around to remind him of their existence. When I was little, I had a child-size card table with two chairs. It was one of my prized possessions and I was saving it for my own children. When my parents were moving away, they brought the set to our house, but I never saw it again. Dennis broke my heart by throwing it away, although he never would admit it. His attitude was so hurtful that when my mom gave me all of her treasured family albums for safekeeping, Dennis managed to slip them out of the house and into the garbage. As a result, I have nothing from my mother's life.

In the '80s I worked part-time for an airline and wore a uniform. My navy-blue pumps had to always shine, so one day I asked Dennis if he would polish them for me. I regret the way I worded my request because I said that my dad had always polished both mine and my mom's boots and shoes. Wrong thing to say. He refused to help me, telling me that I could do them myself. For the next twenty years Dennis made quite a production of shining his shoes at the kitchen table. He'd spread newspaper and towels while setting up his shine kit and spend an hour or two polishing his shoes and ignoring mine.

My dad didn't visit us very often because he knew he wasn't welcome, but Mom came to help when we traveled. Dennis appeared to be very kind to her because she was the only child sitter we could call upon. She didn't charge us and paid for her own plane ticket. When it was time for her to go to the airport, he would insist on taking her and they would often stop for breakfast on the way. He would actually wait until the plane had taken off. Mom thought that was so kind and wonderful of him. She never knew how he really felt about her and that he was just making sure she was gone.

## 17 – Saying Goodbye

When the phone rings in the middle of the night we all know what it means. It's either a wrong number or bad news. On July 10, 1998 when the phone rang at 1:30 a.m. I instinctively knew it wasn't a wrong number.

Things had not been going well for a number of weeks. Mom and Dad had moved into their new condo the year before. That was a huge adjustment for my dad, who always needed to putter and have space to do so. Condo living was not going to be for him. Too much time on his hands would lead to too much drinking. My dad thrived on control of others but when there was no one else around his sole purpose was to control my mom.

It was a Sunday, and they were headed out on their boat to go fishing. A great part of Dad's control was rushing Mom when she wasn't quite ready. There was no rush, but Dad thrived on creating chaos and upsetting her.

On this particular day Mom poured some bleach into her white sink and ran the hot water to fill it up and give it a good cleaning. Dad must have interrupted her to hurry up and get going as they had to get to the boat. I can picture my mom rushing from room to room looking for the things she needed to take. As a result, she forgot to turn off the running water because she couldn't hear it running. She probably couldn't find all the things she needed because that was another part of my dad's scheming. He had been hiding things from her.

My mother's brother Johnny died from complications of Alzheimer's. Mom was very fearful of losing her memory and turning out just like Johnny. She had a very sharp mind and she never forgot anything, so I never held the same fears. If there had been signs of memory loss, I would have picked up on it. She liked to knit and do crafts and recently had begun "misplacing" her knitting needles. One day my dad reached behind the curtains in the family room and said,

"Oh look Audrey, they're here. You must have forgotten where you put them." We both knew he was trying to make her think she was losing her mind.

This was nothing new. A few years previously in 1985, I invited my mom to take a trip with my daughter and me to London, England for a week. I was very specific on the phone before they drove across the prairies to our place. My mom would need her passport and she had to be sure it hadn't expired. Dennis certainly didn't want my dad around, but Dad came anyway to spend the week with Dennis and our son. Mom, Keele and I flew overnight to London and after deplaning proceeded to the lineup for Customs. My mom went to a different line and suddenly I heard her exclaim, "Oh my God!" She was white as a ghost and looked like she was going to collapse. I rushed to her side, only to discover that she did not have her passport but instead she had my dad's. We could have easily been put right back on the plane to return home, but fortunately this was the mid-'80s before terrorism really struck. They could see that my mom who was almost sixty-five was in shock and hadn't planned this. They wrote a letter for her on the spot allowing her into the country. We figured out pretty fast that my dad had switched the passports to get her in trouble and to see her deported.

Several years later my parents flew into town for the Christmas holidays. It was a warm winter, and the snow was melting everywhere, making vehicles very dirty and a leaving a puddle of water at the front door every day. The day before they left, my dad asked to borrow my car for a couple of hours. He returned it with a thank-you and told me he had it washed for me. They next day the car was in our garage and we piled into it to go to the airport. I was driving a new Mercury Sable, the first car I'd ever bought and paid for myself, and I was very proud. When I started it up, in a darkened garage all the dashboard lights were glowing brightly. The car's heating system was all push-button controlled and set with a thermostat. I looked and gasped. All the buttons were smashed. My dad tried to come up with the excuse that I'd broken them all with my long nails... as if. I was furious. I knew he did it because he did not understand the temperature settings and was an extremely impatient and violent person. He's smashed them all, but if I said anything or confronted him, I knew he'd take it out on my mom. I dropped them off at the airport, hardly saying a word, and drove right to the dealership at the top of my street, in tears.

It wasn't until I was married and left home that I learned my dad had been physically abusive towards my mom. This continued even more when they retired and moved away. One summer I was able to get my mom into a women's shelter when she was trying to escape my father's grasp. After that she joined a support group which I hoped would give her the courage to leave, but she stayed with him out of fear. We could see through my dad and his tricks. But years later when she was still seeing a support group, my dad referred to them as "The Society of Widows."

To return to this particular day in June 1998... Dad was rushing mom to get going as he wanted to go fishing. My mom was completely deaf in her right ear, with almost no hearing in her left. As he rushed to get her outside their suite, he would have heard the water running and may have even seen it, but he never mentioned it. The water could run over and there could be a flood, but if there were consequences then he could hold them over her head. He was sick.

After several hours out on the lake they returned home to a flood in their apartment. Imagine the taps running for three to four hours in a double sink that contained hot water and bleach. It overflowed soon after they left, flooding their kitchen and family room, seeping through the floor to the condo below them and eventually the condo below that. A major disaster in their complex. Three floors flooded!

I didn't hear about this for several days, as Mom didn't call me that week. My mom was in such shock that she was shaken to her core. Was Dad supportive of her? Of course not. He phoned everyone he knew and told the story of what Audrey had done. Poor him. He had to deal with all of this. Audrey was losing her memory and her mind. She and she alone had forgotten to turn off the running water.

The damage was extensive but fortunately their insurance covered it in all three condos. It was all Mom's fault, and she was humiliated. But just when you think at the age of seventy-six, she would crumble under the stress, she did the exact opposite. She gained strength, took out the phone book and found a lawyer. She would never be blamed and humiliated again.

I didn't hear about all of this until a few days after the fact. I was a bit stunned that Mom went to see a lawyer at all, let alone one she didn't know. She took with her copies of all their investments and bank statements which she alone looked after. Then she called me to tell me she wanted a divorce after fifty-three years of marriage.

One brave lady.

Their fifty-third wedding anniversary was Tuesday, June 30, and by Friday July 3 she presented Dad with her request for a divorce and the splitting of their assets. My dad could neither read or write and would never be able to function on his own. He had controlled her every move and he would not let her go easily. Mom confided her fears to me, and we decided that it would be best if she left town. I made a plane reservation and assured her that she could stay with me as long as she needed to. She would arrive on Friday, July 10, and I would keep her whereabouts unknown so Dad could not follow.

Dad talked to me only once in that time period, telling me what she had done and the damage she created by flooding the building. Poor him. I wanted to challenge him and say, "I'm sure you could hear or see the water running, why didn't you turn it off?" but I didn't dare. He would take it out on my mom. I could tell he'd been drinking. I phoned him on the Tuesday evening after all Mom's plans were set. He told me that he had poured all his liquor down the sink, although I doubted it. I offered to come and help him. If he was going to give up drinking, he wouldn't be able to do it on his own. "Just say the word, Dad and I will be there." He hung up on me.

The next evening my dad took an overdose of pills, but they didn't work. I believe it was an effort to get attention so my mom would feel guilty and stay. Their neighbor, who was a nurse, came in at my mom's request because she had trouble waking him in the morning. There was no doubt that if he really wanted to kill himself there were enough pills in the bathroom to level a horse. Out of fear and concern the neighbor told my mom to leave—to just pack a few things and go. Since she was already set to leave for Winnipeg on the Friday morning, she quickly packed what she would need and drove to a friend's home. At seventy-six years of age, she had to go into hiding until her flight.

Thursday, July 9 I heard nothing. I had an appointment with my hairdresser on the other side of town, so I took the perimeter highway around the city. There and back. I was nauseous with fear mixed with anger. On my way home I took a moment and pulled off on the side of the road. It was a very typical prairie day, blue sky and sunshine that stretched forever to the west. I looked through the windshield of my car and prayed out loud. "God, make this stop!" I said it over and over, for I knew this had been building my entire life and things were about to explode.

I was in a deep sleep when the phone rang July 10 at 1:30 a.m. on that Friday, and I instinctively knew it was bad news. It was my mom's friend who was temporarily keeping her safe. She said, "The RCMP just called and your dad is gone. They have been looking for your mother. Your dad has taken his life and they will be calling you any minute now." She went on to explain that neighbors heard the gunshot, and when the RCMP arrived there was fear that Dad had taken my mother's life first, then his own. Murder/suicide. Right below their beautiful condo was an apple orchard. He took his life there, under a giant spruce tree that was directly in the view of their living room. I think that location was on purpose. He hoped she would look out at that spot every day and be reminded that he did this. More details would come out after I talked with the RCMP officer. We phoned the kids and booked our flights. We would be on our way to Kelowna even before my mom was awake and aware of what Dad had done. I would soon learn that not everything you lose is a loss.

## 18 – Therapy

Mom and her friends met us at the airport. It was only around nine thirty in the morning, but Mom was already in high gear. Dad's body was being held at the coroner's office. Unbeknownst to me, my dad carried a card in his wallet stating he did not want a funeral. The decision had been made that once his body had been released, he would go directly to the funeral home of our choice where he would be cremated immediately. We learned the RCMP had confiscated all his guns. Not a lot, maybe four or five used for hunting or skeet shooting. They would be released by the afternoon.

In a very strange twist, Dennis wanted to see his body. He needed proof that his father-in-law was indeed dead. He said that he even wanted to see the bullet hole. After years and years of living with the terrible things Dad had done to discredit him in business, who could blame him? We went back to the condo to pick up clothes for Dad to be cremated in. Strangely that was important to me. After all, I was in the fashion business and I did not want him looking like a bum. Remembering that we were all still deep in shock, that now seems really silly.

We went to the funeral home, handed over his clothes and had to make the decision about a casket. Mom clearly wanted him to be put in a cardboard box. Who could blame her? She said she wanted one of the big fish trophy boxes that we used to ship fish in. Dennis and I couldn't do that. Even with decades of anger inside him, Dennis felt we needed to show some respect, and so we chose not the lowest priced but the second lowest priced casket. Back at the condo we found that Dad had left a note and a Chinese fortune cookie. Dad loved Chinese food, so we think that was what he chose for his last meal. We opened the fortune cookie and were stunned by what it said. You know they never really make much sense but this one did. It said, "Your next purchase will be a good deal." How insightful that my mom's next purchase would be the second lowest priced casket and no funeral costs. That was indeed a deal. I will never doubt a fortune cookie again.

We returned to the funeral home in the afternoon. It was time to view the body and say our goodbyes. The casket, with Dad in it, was at the front of the chapel. The chapel was huge. I felt as if I was in a church. No one could have predicted what came next, and I can't remember who went first. We sat in one of the front pews. Dennis, Mom and I each took our turns. Over and over, we walked around the casket, staring down at Dad and telling him exactly what we thought of him and what he had done to each of us. He looked like he was asleep. Since the body had not been embalmed, nothing about his look had changed. I brought a nice shirt and pair of pants for him to be dressed in, and during one of my trips around the coffin I stuffed my business card into his breast pocket. Just in case he wanted to phone or write and apologize from the other side, he had my number.

I have no idea what Mom or Dennis said, as I was too deep in my own anger, and dumping it all right there and then was my mission. We took turns at this for forty-five or so minutes, resting in a front pew while the next one took a turn. It felt like forever and it felt fantastic to be able to unload my feelings and to say all of the things that had built up over the years. I had never figured out how to say them until that moment.

It was time to go and as we walked down the long aisle to the double door exit, I had an idea. I said to my mom, "You have a choice, Mom. You've just experienced about ten years of therapy. You can leave all that pain and anger here, or you can take it with you and drag it around with you for the rest of your life. The decision is yours." As we approached the end of the aisle Mom began sweeping her arms backwards and repeatedly said, "Back, stay back... shoo you, stay back." She was trying to keep all that bad energy she had just dumped from following her into the real world. In that moment the funeral director opened the double doors. I can't imagine what he thought, but I know what he saw, and he probably thought we were all nuts. Mom and I giggled ourselves silly.

Since Dad didn't want a funeral it seemed more appropriate to have a happy hour in his honor, and that is what we did. I made the hors d'oeuvres and we hauled down all Dad's liquor to the party room in their complex. All Mom and Dad's closest friends were invited. Sadly, Mom didn't get a card or a flower from anyone. We learned after that Dad had canceled his golf game for July 10 and had been crying to friends that Audrey was losing her memory and her mind, and he was the one suffering. Everyone blamed Mom for her husband's suicide.

Within a week there was very little trace that my dad had ever lived there. We sold his bedroom suite and gave all his clothes to charity. We sold the boat against Mom's wishes, but we had a buyer, and we knew she was too old to handle taking a boat out on a big lake. Both our children had flown in for a few days and they helped us get rid of everything. We had to decide where to spread Dad's ashes—from the boat seemed a logical place because he loved the lake so much. But he never took mechanical care of anything, and upon thinking about the worse-case scenario, we realized that if we all went out on the lake to spread his ashes, the boat might stall, and we could be adrift for days. Or the wind would blow the ashes back on us. He was just that kind of guy. None of that was sitting with us very well, so instead we spread them in the orchard where he had taken his life.

Much to our surprise, when we picked up the guns from the RCMP, my dad's favorite shotgun had a note to my son Damien on it. He was the only one who got a goodbye. My dad had an old Toyota truck and my mom wanted my son Damien to have it. We bought new tires, had the engine tuned up and Damien headed back to Winnipeg in his grandpa's truck. I stayed an extra week to help Mom. We bought new dishes, bedding and towels. We turned Dad's bedroom into TV room with a new couch. I cleaned out cupboards and did a lot of rearranging, because that is what I do when I am stressed. But in the end, I had to change the kitchen cupboards back to their original setup. Mom was much shorter than me and she couldn't reach a thing.

My dad's truck was around for a very long time. Damien inherited it in 1998 but in 2001 his sister Keele was moving out West and he gave it to her. When she was planning her wedding in the summer of 2004, I was there to help her. Keele's SUV was in for repair so we had to drive the truck everywhere, including the beautiful restaurant where the wedding reception would be. We ate lunch there one day to test the menu and when it was time to pay the bill, there wasn't one. I joked that management probably saw the dump of a truck we pulled up in and thought we couldn't afford to pay. A few days later on the way to the airport, Keele questioned me in a bit of a snip about my attitude towards the old truck. My answer was simple. "If your dad had used this vehicle to kill himself, you wouldn't want to drive in it either." You see, my dad had put his shotgun on the back bumper. With a stick that had a nail in it, he aimed the barrel at his chest and pushed the stick so that the nail would set off the trigger. I watched in that moment as Keele's color drained from her face. In hindsight I realized that we had never told the kids how grandpa killed himself. She was stunned and I felt very bad for catching her off guard. After she dropped me at the airport, I never saw the truck again.

Shortly after Dad's death and right after we returned home, there was a call at the office from one of my dad's old cronies. Fortunately, Dennis was out of the office and couldn't take the call. This friend of Dad's said Dennis must now be thrilled that he had finally inherited the family business through me. We bought the business from my parents in 1975 and had my parents paid in full by 1985. But Dad still had told everyone he owned it. He had to always be the big shot and have the final word.

## 19 – Searching for an Answer

By the spring of 1997 we began many changes in our life. Because I knew that Dennis had been clean for six months, I no longer had doubts about him, and my trust issues were minimized.

We made the decision to sell our big dream home and downsize. Our children were gone, and we didn't need all that space anymore. We had fallen in love with a townhouse development from a distance. It was four levels, modern and on a beautiful creek. We were able to find a unit that suited us and moved in on August 30. I honestly felt so much stress and unhappiness in our home. I had hoped that a move to a happier place, one without bad memories would make our lives easier. It was the best decision we could have made but my fevers raged on.

I had now done all the allergy testing possible and it was thought I might have developed an environmental allergy. Really, we were grasping at straws. The last place you want to spend New Year's Eve is the emergency room of a major hospital, but that is where I was on that night in 1997. We had picked up dinner at our favorite restaurant and planned a quiet evening at home, but I could feel one of my fevers starting and we headed to the ER. It must have been minus twenty outside but my doctor had suggested that with my next fever I go to the ER so I could be tested for malaria. We were there about four hours and of course I didn't have malaria. Over the next twelve months I was tested four different times.

By September of 1998, with my dad now gone, I had some money to invest in my health, so Dennis and I headed south to Rochester, Minnesota and the world-renowned Mayo Clinic.

I'd taken my mom to the Mayo Clinic in the early '90s for her macular degeneration, so I knew how things worked. It really was like checking into the Ritz-Carlton Hotel. I was booked for five days of testing. They were going to turn me inside out. We stayed at a lovely small hotel just down the street so that I could rest during the day. Dennis was a different person now. He was so kind to me and absolutely worried sick while waiting for my results. At times he almost had to carry me from one test to the next. I had a full-blown fever while I was there so the doctors could see firsthand what I was going through. When I was too weak to go back to our hotel, Dennis would just lay me down in the lobby and I would sleep for an hour or two.

By the time you go to the Mayo Clinic the doctors presume you've exhausted all avenues at home, which I felt we had. After five days of tests and two days of killing time waiting for results, we sat down to hear the news.

I had asthma, acid reflux and a rare Mediterranean fever that is found in Greeks and Arabs. Well, I knew I didn't have asthma, they didn't tell me what acid reflux was, and as far as the Mediterranean fever, I am a Minnesota Norwegian by my roots, and I didn't know how that was possible. They gave me several "puffers" with directions for when and how to use them. That was it except for the bill, which was almost $16,000 Canadian.

We checked out of our hotel to begin the eight-hour drive home when Dennis got a terrible dizzy spell that almost knocked him off his feet. The stress of that week just about leveled him, and I was the one who had to take the wheel. On the drive home he confessed to me that although he really wasn't religious, he'd spent the week praying that God would take him and make me better. A reminder to be careful of what you ask for.

Back home I took my results to my internist who was somewhat suspicious of their findings. He explained that the medicine they suggested for the Mediterranean fever could actually kill me. For weeks I had to return to the hospital and have "live" blood drawn from me, which was sent to the CDC in Atlanta. I really was getting tremendous care even if the results were slim. I never heard from the CDC, but my internist reminded me that eventually something would surface and give us an answer. We just had to be patient.

Still afraid that my illness could be environmental, I stayed away from older buildings and homes. I didn't go out much. I even had a personal trainer who would come weekly to my home. I continued to build my business by working more from my home, and I planned life around my fevers. I would burn up with fever, then sweat profusely for two days while I felt I was coughing up a lung. Every time I saw my doctor, he reminded me that I wasn't dead yet. He felt that eventually the cause would present itself.

## 20 – Life Changing

One morning my mom called to tell me about a made-for-TV movie she had watched. It was the story of a man who discovered late in life that he had Attention Deficit Hyperactivity Disorder (ADHD). My dad had never learned to read or write, and Mom and I always wondered if he had a learning disability, in spite of the fact that he was a very smart man. Mom wondered aloud if that was what had been the matter with Dad. I brought the subject up with Dennis simply because he too was never still. Even when relaxing, his leg was always shaking or his fingers tapping. Dennis was open to the possibility that he could have a learning disability and wanted to be tested.

When I say "life changing" I truly mean it. According to the psychologist who tested Dennis, his ADHD was so extreme that she didn't know how he'd reached the age of fifty-one without putting a gun to his head. That's extreme, but it became the turning point in his new life. The dialogue was started, and those layers began to peel away some more. Dennis now understood what had been happening to him his entire life. He became an advocate for ADD and ADHD and he joked that every entrepreneur in our industry suffered from it. He photocopied copious amounts of information which he always kept on hand ready to hand out. He was reading for the first time in our twenty-five years together. He talked, he shared, he opened up. Most importantly, for the first time he talked about the son he lost. We both went to the psychologist together and I saw and heard firsthand how much pain he had been in for almost thirty years. People make decisions based on their emotions and do not think of the consequences in the present and certainly not in the future. The choice his son's mother made so many years ago had tremendous consequences and effects on Dennis. He confessed that the pain was so great that doing drugs was a way of dealing and masking his feelings. He admitted he had been committing slow suicide to cover up his pain. I have never been prouder of him. We had been to marriage therapy about four different times in twenty-six years and not once had the subject of losing a child come to the surface, or that he had been divorced. Now it was out, raw, and Dennis was healing right before my eyes.

Dennis also joined CA, which stands for Cocaine Anonymous. At first, I was horrified, again because of the embarrassment. What if someone we knew saw him there? I realized this wasn't about me when I began to see his joy in doing the twelve steps. His partner at CA was a former biker—a huge man who surprisingly had the same last name as Dennis's mother before she was married. Dennis joked that they were cousins, and he formed a strong bond with the man who would help him.

I was never invited to take part. I was fine with that because I knew he was doing the steps. He never missed a meeting. This was his thing and I watched him closely and was encouraged daily by his growth. I was never quite sure how far he went in the program because I knew there were two important steps that should have involved me. These two steps were 1) Make a list of all persons he had harmed, and 2) Make direct amends to such people wherever possible, except when to do so would injure them or others. There should have been an apology coming to me but there never was. I never knew if he got to the second step.

Dennis by nature was an extremely generous person and I was concerned that his generosity could be taken advantage of. He gave possessions away, sometimes without asking, which didn't make me happy. But this was a new man, and I could see and experience the joy in his heart. I never felt closer to him or loved him more.

## 21 – Suspicion and Solution

In July of 1999 my mom and I took a Mediterranean cruise and a two-week bus tour of Italy. It was the first anniversary of Dad's suicide and I felt Mom and I needed to be kept busy. I took hundreds of pictures and on our return, I asked Dennis if he would like to see them. He never answered and never asked, so I never bothered to try again. Dennis had been recovering and our lives were just starting to settle down, when he suddenly began to act strangely, in some ways similar yet somehow different from the behavior of his cocaine days.

A few weeks after my return from Italy, we went to Calgary for a conference; I drove because I knew the way to our downtown hotel. Dennis was furious when I went in the wrong direction and the route took us a little longer. It just didn't make sense why he would be so mad. The next day while I was in classes he went shopping and bought me two beautiful gifts as an apology. He said he didn't know what had gotten into him and he was so sorry.

Before we left the city, we stopped at a local mall to shop a bit. We had a specific time and place where we were to meet. Dennis never showed up. Instead, I found him wandering around the store as if he had all the time in the world and nowhere else to be.

A month later my Aunt Gladys passed away and I spoke at her funeral. At the reception following, Dennis just stayed in the hall outside. He wouldn't come in for refreshments. What was his problem? Later that month I was hosting a big fashion show and needed him to sit down and number all the tickets for me. Luckily, I checked them when he was done. I found that the numbers were all out of sequence and many had to be redone.

By October he just got more and more strange. He didn't like the food I was cooking. He complained that clean laundry smelled awful, and I had to go into the basement to paint my nails because he couldn't stand the smell. I'd been painting my nails in his presence for almost thirty years. I didn't understand what was happening to him. So, no more spices and no more fabric softener. Then he said he could hear the TV in the condo next door and banged on the wall like some grumpy old man. I was horrified.

Could he be using cocaine again? I couldn't deal with that. I had no proof, but I was very worried. I couldn't ask and I didn't want to spy, but I knew something wasn't right.

## 22 – A Miracle of my Own

In the midst of Dennis getting stranger I had found a miracle of my own. I returned to my internist with a question. Why, if I was so healthy in spite of my fevers, was I able to feel the entire outline of my stomach? It burned twenty-four hours a day. I didn't seem to have any food issues, but my gut felt like it was on fire.

My doctor asked what I was taking for my acid reflux as diagnosed by the Mayo Clinic. Nothing. I told him they hadn't prescribed anything for me. I didn't even know what acid reflux was.

He prescribed a little purple pill that nowadays is advertised on TV and sold over the counter. I started taking one at bedtime and I've never, ever, had another fever attack.

The acid in my stomach had built up so much that it shot up my esophagus and spilled over into my lungs. Hence the never-ending cough that caused me to vomit all the time. My body was at war, fighting off the invasion into my lungs. My body temperature would rise to 104 °F to fight off that invasion and infection. It's a disease called Gastroesophageal Reflux Disease or GERD.

In surveys, the majority of people who experience acid reflux identify stress as a common trigger. The problem is that studies have failed to find a connection between the stress and the amount of stomach acid in the esophagus, which is the ultimate cause of heartburn pain.

Four and a half years of agony and it was over. How many times did I tell a doctor that I was living with catastrophic stress? Perhaps the dots could have been connected if just one doctor had really listened. Our minds, our bodies and our emotions are all connected, and my secrets were truly making me sick.

Although I had lost so much time that I would never get back, did I stay in bed whining and playing the victim? Certainly not. With two phone lines into our home and two puppies at my feet, I built a million-dollar business from my bed.

## 23 – Millennium

The twentieth century and 1999 was drawing to a close. I wanted a big celebration with my family simply because this would never happen again in our lifetime. Besides, the world just might end at midnight on December 31, so why not party together and ring in a new century while the curtain was being drawn?

I wanted to treat Dennis and the children to a week in Mexico, but Dennis was not excited about the prospect of a trip and wanted us all to stay home. My mom would come up from Arizona, where she had her winter home, for Christmas and the New Year. She would look after the dogs while we partied at a fancy hotel with a group of our friends.

All I wanted for Christmas was my two front teeth—literally. I had decided to have my front teeth fixed because they were crooked. This was a huge deal for me because I don't like going to the dentist. At the beginning of the month Dennis was away on business but called me with encouragement the night before my dental appointment. He was very supportive as he knew this was something I really wanted, I just needed to be brave. On his return home I smiled big smiles with my temporary caps, fishing for a compliment, but I didn't get one.

A week later when the permanent crowns were on, he didn't ask to see or even mention it. I remember driving to the dentist that morning and seeing Dennis driving right behind me. When I stopped at a red light, I looked in my rearview mirror to see that Dennis wasn't even slowing down. I really thought he was going to rear end me in his big F150 truck, but he slammed on the brakes in time. He didn't even seem to notice that it was me in front of him. Just another one of his weird things. I threw my hands up in the air and exclaimed "MEN!" I tried to avoid thinking about drugs. I couldn't face it if he slipped backwards and certainly not at Christmas.

We have no real Christmas traditions in our family, so my mom, daughter, Dennis and I went out for Chinese food on Christmas Eve. Our son decided to go skiing. At the end of our dinner, when the bill came, Dennis said he couldn't sign his name. His hand just wouldn't work. He walked our daughter to her car, and she suggested that he look into getting his brain scanned after Christmas.

The next morning Dennis woke up really sick to his stomach and unable to get out of bed. He missed Christmas dinner at his sister's home, but we brought some dinner back for him. He could not eat. I actually breathed a sigh of relief. Many people were sick with a flu that Christmas and now Dennis had it too. In a few days he would be okay, and with any luck my mom and I would not get it. To be safe I slept in the den away from him. By Wednesday Dennis wasn't much better. He still wasn't eating, and it became obvious that he'd lost quite a bit of weight. I called a mobile doctor service because I knew he wouldn't be up to partying on New Year's Eve. A doctor made a house call and declared that Dennis was now on the better side of the flu but he would write a letter so we could get a refund on our New Year's party. Although Dennis was getting better the doctor assured us that he wouldn't be in the mood for a party.

The 1900s came to an end with my mom and me parked in front of the TV for twenty-four hours. We watched the celebrations around the world, and it was fabulous to see. Our world had survived. I don't think it even registered with Dennis that it was a new year, let alone a new century. Saturday morning, he got up, showered and said he felt much, much better. We went for a short drive and returned some movies we'd rented. This flu had really wiped him out, but he was now on the mend.

Sunday, January 2 arrived, and things went downhill very fast. Dennis started vomiting again and while on his hands and knees he hollered at me to "Get a medic, get a medic!" I freaked out because the word "medic" is something our generation never uses, and I was frightened. After looking in the phone book for a clinic that might be open, I decided to take Dennis right to Emergency at Grace Hospital. He could barely walk, and at first sight the nurse thought he might have had a stroke. They suggested that because I lived so close, I should go home and come back in two hours. They wanted to do some tests and were very short-staffed.

I won't forget what I did once I got home. I needed to keep busy and kill time so I decided I could do that by taking down the Christmas tree. That would keep me busy for an hour or so, but it was not the job I usually do. Dennis was fanatic about arranging the lights and decorations so they would be easy to pull out the next Christmas. He was a great organizer of all things he deemed important, and Christmas decorations were near the top of the list. It was a great stress reliever for me just to be distracted while he was in the ER and I remember saying to my mom, "I'll be in big shit next year when Dennis sees the mess, I've made of this!"

I returned to the ER two hours later, and to my horror, as I pulled up, I could see Dennis was being loaded into an ambulance. They needed to take him downtown to the Health Sciences Centre where they had additional technology for more tests. I got on my cell phone and as I drove, I phoned everyone who should be notified, then screamed at the top of my lungs the rest of the way there. It didn't take them long to look at Dennis. Keele and a good friend had arrived, as well as Damien, who was just back from his ski trip. Dennis had a brain tumor. Shock! Denial. Then more shock.

Positive self-talk goes a long way at a time like this: he'll be okay... they know what it is... he's very strong... they can do surgery and he'll be as good as new....

It all goes through your head at the same time. Dennis would spend the night back at the Grace Hospital. Monday, MRI machines around the world were being tested for millennium bugs. He would have to wait until Tuesday for his final diagnosis. I counted my blessings and said out loud, "Thank God we're not in Mexico." Dennis was right about insisting we stay at home for the millennium.

Monday was a blur. My mom wanted to see Dennis, as she was flying back to Arizona on Tuesday morning. I dropped her off at the hospital because I had a sales meeting to host. They gave Dennis a massive dose of prednisone, which I didn't think was a good idea. It seemed they didn't know he'd been an addict. Then again, he'd been in their ER five years previously, so maybe they did know. Whatever the case, he seemed as if he was flying high and his attitude was very positive.

Tuesday morning, January 4, 2000, the plan was to drop my mom at the airport and then meet Dennis back at the hospital when he would be getting his MRI and more X-rays. It must have been minus twenty, and since I had a little bit of time, I decided to drop into Costco near the airport. I carried my purchases out to the car, only to discover that I had locked my keys inside. I never, ever do that. Clearly, I should not have been driving that day, as my stress level was at its max. I called a cab. It took forever. I went to the college where my daughter was, to get her house keys, then back to my house to get my other set of car keys, and then back to my car. By the time I'd finished all that, there was no time to go to the Health Sciences Centre, but I would probably be in time for Dennis's return to the Grace Hospital. I parked the car and ran in just as Dennis was being wheeled down the hall. Thank God I had caught up with him.

Completely out of breath, I told the attendant pushing him about my locked car episode and that today couldn't get worse. She never blinked or even looked at me, and I had this terrible, terrible feeling. As Dennis was being lifted onto his bed, a nurse came and told me there was a call for me from the doctor. I remember them pushing a chair behind me as my knees buckled. Dennis had lung cancer and it had already spread to his esophagus and his brain. They could buy him a few months, but Dennis was going to die.

Splat!

## 24 – Hanging on for Dear Life

When you're dead, you're dead. That's what Dennis believed in spite of his Catholic upbringing. There was no heaven, no hell, you are simply here and then you're not. I couldn't believe that. I refused to believe that. This man who had come so far in such a short period of time couldn't suddenly stop being, and it felt like my heart was being ripped out at the very thought of it. That's when I came up with a plan. We would pick a word, one that no one else could guess, and when Dennis got to the other side, he would send me a sign and it would be the word we chose together. Did I believe that could be done? Weird unexplained things have happened to me more than a few times in my life. Did I dare to dream that Dennis could reach out to me once he was gone? No, I was grasping at straws and clinging to hope.

Life had stopped. Dennis came home from the hospital with a list. Medications to take daily and a schedule of radiation appointments. He would not be in pain at any time and that was a huge relief.

How do you live as normal when nothing in your life is? Dennis wanted to return to work. Damien had graduated with his business degree the previous spring and was working with his dad to learn how to run a small business. Now time was of the essence because time was running out. Dennis had twenty-five years of knowledge to impart to our son. Damien would be running the family business, and not by choice, but out of necessity.

Once you know that you are dying there are still more blows to come. First Dennis had to give up his driver's license, something he'd had since he was sixteen. That was a terrible adjustment for him. He was losing his independence. The radiation sickness was the worst. It was horrible and he was so brave. We both knew that it was just buying us time. There was no cure. Then there was his hair. Dennis went silver very prematurely, and his hair was thick and beautiful. We were told it would fall out after the radiation, but it wasn't happening. His hair was fine, thick and as beautiful as ever. A few days after we admired it, he woke up one morning and it all fell out. I took him to a barber shop to have the last wisps shaved off and we marveled at what a beautifully shaped, unblemished head he had.

And my heart broke.

Life at home was very quiet. The goal was to just get through each day. I think we ate more Chinese food than we had in thirty years. Winnipeg is famous for a particular birthday cake made at Jeannie's Bakery, and we ate one a week for several months. Dennis's best buddy, Ron, would drop off our Chinese every few days from our favorite restaurant at the other end of town. That's when I learned a big lesson. As a wife I only wanted what was best for my husband, in every way, but I didn't know what was best in every new circumstance. One night I made the decision not to order wonton soup, a new item Dennis had decided to add. I was afraid the plastic container might leak or spill or open in our friend's car. But It was not my decision to make, and Dennis was beyond furious. I mean he was shaking and crying as if I had committed a huge sin. I hid in the laundry room, humiliated and sobbing. I needed some help.

I really didn't know how to cope, so I found a therapist, but it wasn't the right solution for me. I had to look good, drive across town, cry my eyes out, write a cheque, then try to drive home totally shaken up. I reached out to someone I knew in the Toronto area whom I'd done some training with. I could sit on the floor in my office, in my housecoat with a box of tissues, and pour out my heart on the phone. The first thing I learned was that Dennis was to make all decisions. Every single one, because they were his last. Even if it was just wonton soup.

I was also struggling with a nightmare I had before Dennis got sick. My dad had been dead about a year when I had a horrible dream that I was on the phone and there was a "party line" on the other end. We had to share phone lines in the '50s. We could often hear another person on the line when we picked up the phone to dial out. My dad was the other party in this dream, and I heard him say, "They think I'm dead but I'm not. I'm coming back to take them one at a time." I woke up screaming and Dennis jumped up too. I was on my feet and running and he feared that I was going to run out and off our third-level balcony.

I admit I had been dealing with a lot for five years and I'd had more than my share of real-life nightmares. As strange as it may sound, I needed some confirmation that it wasn't all connected. I needed to know that my dad wasn't reaching out from beyond the grave to punish us all by taking Dennis too.

Mid-February I had to go to Toronto for a conference. Keele came to stay with her dad and one of our good friends came over to cook for him. I was still holding it all in but on the awards night, something triggered inside me. It was a formal evening and many of my team had traveled to Toronto with me. We had done over $1 million in sales and I would be recognized on stage. But, sitting in the audience, it all just hit me, and I started to cry, weeping uncontrollably. With only a small evening bag I really had no tissues, so everyone in my row was passing them down to me. I couldn't stop. Once backstage someone tried to help me, but toilet paper was all they could find. I bet I had ten yards of toilet paper shoved up the sleeve and down the front of my black velvet dress. In every photo that night my face was bright red, and my eyes were almost swollen shut.

During and after his radiation treatments Dennis spent a lot of time in bed sleeping or watching TV. That's when he discovered The Shopping Channel. I don't know just how many things he ordered over time, but I do remember every person in the family got a rosary or two.

Valentine's Day was something we always celebrated, so this year was no exception. Our daughter, Keele, had a boyfriend she wanted us to meet. It would turn out to be her future husband, and I am so delighted that Dennis got to meet him. It was a pleasant evening at one of our favorite restaurants. I was so worried that Dennis would catch a cold now that he had no hair. As well, I had great difficulty eating, since I had been to the dentist that day, and with my frozen mouth I had bitten through my tongue.

It had now been a few years since Dennis had written to his son, John, and sent him the letter with photos. I had not heard if Dennis had a reply, and I felt that the next few months would be his last opportunity to find his first-born. I asked Dennis if he wanted me to search for John. He said no, it was too late now. But it kept eating at me. That young man could have and would have been my stepson. I phoned the therapist we had seen together who knew Dennis's story. I needed her input, but she paused and said that was a very big question and she would call me in twenty-four hours. The next day she called me back and I could tell she was very upset. I knew she was right but so saddened by what she said: "Adele, this is not your story, so you cannot interfere." I had to respect the advice I'd been given even though it hurt tremendously.

In April Dennis appeared to regain some strength. He wanted to go on a trip, one last time. We talked about New Orleans but decided it was too far. Then we considered Ottawa. I even bought the tickets, but they were never used. We settled on a short road trip with his sister, Mary-Jane, and her husband, Doug, to Grand Forks, North Dakota. We really had a good time. A little shopping and great dinners out. Everything was fine until the trip home and our crossing at the border. We had a small amount to declare and Dennis went to one customs officer and I went to the other. I didn't have a clue how much his brain and thinking process was in peril. Fortunately, the officer who was looking after him could tell and processed him very quickly, but once back in the car Dennis let me have it. How could I have abandoned him like that? He needed help and I wasn't there for him. I was almost sick to my stomach and the water works started again. I sat in the front seat and quietly cried the rest of the way home.

We had two big events to attend before Dennis would go into palliative care. One weekend one of our staff got married. We didn't go to the service but got all dressed up and went to the dinner and reception. The air was blue with cigarette smoke, but Dennis said it was okay and he simply wanted to be there. Throughout the evening Dennis was approached by each one of our staff and their wives or husbands. It was truly touching how they knelt down beside him or pulled up a chair to be close. This would be the last time he would see many of them. Our staff was very long-term, and some had been with us over twenty-five years. I couldn't go near as it was too heartbreaking. Dennis cared so deeply for so many, and in turn it was almost as if they were kneeling, in respect, before the Godfather.

The second event was even more difficult. A friend of Dennis was being inducted into the Canadian Aviation Hall of Fame and he and his wife invited us to the dinner. Dennis was really starting to weaken at this point, but he was delighted to be included and we sat at a table for ten. It was a lovely evening, but when you don't know anyone and there are ten at a round table it is extremely difficult to have a conversation with anyone. Of course, everyone knew that Dennis was dying.

We were invited to another dinner with the same group the next evening. A private room was reserved for our group in one of the city's best restaurants. I knew that was taxing Dennis to the limit, but he insisted on going because, as he said, it would be the last time he saw this group of friends. It was so fantastic to hear him laughing all evening as stories were told. And I was told one of the best stories of my life.

A woman from another city who sat across from me the night before approached me and said, "I have been where your husband is going." I didn't have a clue what she meant, so she proceeded to tell me her story and I felt the hair on the back of my neck stand on end. Thirty years before, she had died on the delivery table giving birth to her son. She was suddenly looking at herself in labor but from above. Then in an instant she was in a field of flowers, all colors and none she recognized. Her father, who had died when she was a child, was running towards her calling her name. She said he wasn't speaking but her mind could read what he said. He wanted her to follow him, but she turned and looked back from where she came. At that moment her son was born and instinctively, although she knew something wasn't right, she was overwhelmed with a feeling of love. She knew her son would not survive without a mother's love. In an instant she was brought back to life and her view of heaven had vanished. Her son was born mentally handicapped and today was living independently, employed and happy. She told me that he was her purpose in her life and she was so very proud of him. Her story gave me the hope I was needing.

By May 2 Dennis was really starting to decline. I took him to the ER, and he was diagnosed with pneumonia. Also, the shingles rash was creeping across his forehead. I called for some in-home nursing help, as I no longer felt strong enough to deal with the situation alone. A nurse came daily, but after two weeks it became clear that it was too dangerous to have him at home. We lived in a four-level home and the open concept stairs had me terrified of a fall. There was also the fear that Dennis could have a seizure.

I recall that Monday, May 22 was the date chosen to go to palliative care, and I honestly do not know how Dennis managed those last few days at home. It was absolutely heartbreaking and horrible. On the Sunday we went to The Pancake House for our favorite breakfast with his sister and her husband. Then that evening he had me take him for a drive. He wanted to see, for the very last time, the homes he'd grown up in, our first apartment, the business, and the two homes we had owned. The last thing he decided on was a soft ice cream. Oh, how he loved ice cream. He could only handle a few licks and he was very tired. It was time to go home for one last night.

## 25 – The Eye of the Tiger

Dennis and I truly believed in organ donation, which was something we had noted on our driver's licenses. In case of sudden death, a hospital could proceed. When someone is dying from cancer there is no opportunity for that wish. I knew that but still held out hope that we could do something, even though at that point Dennis and I had not discussed it. I asked one of the palliative care nurses about corneal donation and transplant and she said she would look into it for me. Almost immediately I got a letter from the Lions Eye Bank of Winnipeg. This is their mission: "to maintain professional staff to procure (remove), process, and distribute human donor eye tissue for surgical transplantation in recipients of Manitoba and Northwest Ontario, as well as providing tissue for surgical training and for medical research."

The letter thanked me for contacting them, but they were very sorry to say that no part of a cancer patient could be used for transplant. There was, however, a way for us to help. People are very aware of donating corneas but not educated on the fact that entire eyes are needed for research. If we chose to donate an entire eye of Dennis's, it would be greatly appreciated. I couldn't and wouldn't do that.

Dennis was known for three specific things. His "silver fox" hair, his outrageous laugh, and his big beautiful blue eyes. It was his eyes that attracted me first. As much as they may be needed, I could not donate an entire eye of his. I started to cry. My own mother had macular degeneration. Both Dennis and our son were born with a lazy eye. Research is ongoing and necessary; still, I could not bring myself to sign the forms. Instead, I put them in the drawer of his hospital nightstand and closed it. This was just too much to do.

About a week later, on a very rainy day, some good friends were in town to spend time with Dennis. They told me to take a break from the hospital, and I needed it. One day when I had taken Dennis to the ER,

I saw a beautiful picture of an Italian fountain hanging on the wall. It reminded me of my trip to Italy with my mom the summer before. I decided that on my afternoon away I would go in search of that picture, so I could hang it somewhere in my home. I drove to a local art gallery to see what they had and tried to describe the picture. The moment I walked through their door into the building I was stopped in my tracks. There, across the showroom to my right, on the floor and leaning against a table, was an unframed painting of a tiger that had me mesmerized. I was drawn to it as if nothing else was in the room. I couldn't stop staring and I knew that I had to have that painting.

I stood there fixed on the tiger, unable to move, when someone asked me if they could help. I asked about the painting and if it was for sale. I also mentioned that I would not be taking it now, that my husband was in palliative care and I wanted this painting in the future. Could they put it on hold for me until the time was right?

I will never forget the woman who looked after me. She took the painting over to the counter and I followed. She explained that she was a fairly recent widow and that her husband had died in his sleep. In that moment we bonded as if we'd known each other for years. We both welled up with tears. She told me how lucky I was to have whatever time was left to say my goodbyes. I told her how lucky she was that she didn't have to watch her husband suffer and disappear. We just stood there staring at each other, locked in our pain.

They could hold this precious piece of art for me as long as I needed them to. I simply wanted it to be mine. She took my credit card to the back room to take my deposit, then came back with the receipt and some very powerful words of wisdom. She told me that the tiger in the painting was moving forward with great force, in a blaze of sunlight, through a shallow stream. She noted how the spray of water around him depicted the strength of his stride. As if by divine direction she told me, "You too will move your life forward with each new step, and with the same determination and resolve as the tiger." Then she added, "Did you ever see a tiger with such big blue eyes?"

That was it. I knew instantly what I had to do. This was a gift, like a sign from above. I immediately returned to the hospital and my husband's room. There I took the paperwork from the nightstand drawer and I signed my name donating Dennis's eyes, knowing in my heart it was the right thing to do, without a split second of regret.

## 26 – Happy Crappy Birthday

I was about to turn fifty. That's a milestone. I certainly won't forget an earlier milestone, my fortieth birthday. I had a complete breakdown in the meat department at Safeway that morning when a distant memory flashed back. It was the memory of my mom's fortieth birthday at our cottage. She wanted to waterski, and when we got her up and out of the water, all the kids on the shoreline and the dock cheered because they got "the old lady" up on skis. Now I was the old lady.

Dennis mastered a total surprise for me on my fortieth. My parents came for a visit to help me celebrate and Dennis booked a table at Hy's Restaurant, our favorite, for a family dinner. That was all I expected, so it was quite a shock when I was directed into a private dining room that was filled with the couples who meant the most to me. My cousin and her husband had even flown in from Toronto for the event. It was spectacular—Dennis had roses for all the ladies and a giant bouquet for me as well. But the most special gift was an autographed football from the Winnipeg Blue Bombers team of 1989. Since Dennis had never been a football fan, this was indeed a very special and thoughtful present and I loved it. Turning forty was wonderful.

Turning fifty in the palliative care ward was a nightmare. Such a nightmare that I didn't celebrate another birthday until I was sixty-one. There were certain days that Dennis could not die. June 9 was one of them. That was my fiftieth birthday and Dennis, even before he went to the hospital, had planned for it to be special. God bless the man for trying and for being so thoughtful. It's one birthday I will never forget—although I wish I could.

Dennis was very excited about the gift for my fiftieth, something he had Birks Jewelers order from their Montreal store and ship in. After his death I went to the store to thank the staff for their care and participation in making it all happen, and we shed a few tears together. Although they had never met Dennis, they thought he was a wonderful, thoughtful man.

My gift was a beautiful crystal bowl. Solid crystal, about eighteen inches in diameter, with a solid sterling silver disk floating in the bottom. Dennis had it engraved with a saying that was special to us: "I love you more today than yesterday and less than tomorrow." We had had this same saying engraved in our wedding bands.

I recall opening my gift in the afternoon, then our children picked up Chinese food and a small cake for dinner. The plan was to eat together in Dennis's room, but because of his brain tumors and his acute sense of smell, we had to move the party down to the family room at the end of the hall. That didn't work out either. After only a few minutes Dennis had to go back to his room because now we made the family room stink as well. We sat eating in silence. The tension and sadness made swallowing difficult.

I took my gift home that day because it was large and breakable, and I didn't want to risk having it around a hospital room. The next morning Dennis said, "I remember giving you a present, but I don't remember what it was. Could you please bring it back?" This went on for two more days until he forgot completely.

Twenty years later, that crystal bowl has now seen four different homes and still holds a place of honor. Not only was it thoughtful and beautiful, it was expensive, $1600. How do I know? Three weeks after Dennis died, his Visa bill came, and I had to pay for it.

## 27 – Counting Down

There were other days when Dennis could not die. After he lived through my birthday he couldn't die on Father's Day. That would make that yearly event more painful than we could bear. Then there was June 29, Keele's birthday, and July 4, Damien's birthday. I was adamant about those dates, as if you can plan death.

I spent every night at the Grace Hospital since Dennis was admitted except for the first night. It broke my heart to leave him there hidden behind a curtain, sharing the room with another terminally ill man, knowing he was there to die, and I was able to go home. We were praying for a private room, but then someone else would have to die for us to get one. The very next morning we had our private room.

I alternated between an old couch in the corner and an air mattress on the floor. The air mattress offered little comfort because the cold vinyl flooring made the air in the mattress cold and I was really suffering from back pain. It didn't help that I'd had a big fall in the parking lot. While running in the rain to reach my car, the gravel under my feet began to roll and I flew through the air and onto my hip and left arm before I could catch or save myself. I was at the chiropractor every other day to get some relief, so sleeping on a lumpy couch or a cold floor made it all worse.

Keele was working and tried to come every evening for a visit or spend the night and give me a break. Damien rarely came. He was trying to run a business, and seeing his dad wasting away was far too difficult for him. On Wednesday, June 23, neither Keele nor I stayed the night. It was only the second time in a month that Dennis had been on his own. Keele had a touch of the flu and I needed one good sleep. The phone rang at 5 a.m. Dennis had fallen. I rushed to the hospital not knowing what to expect. Dennis was so terribly thin and weak that now walking on his own was impossible. He was trying to get to the bathroom. It would be the last time he was out of bed.

He was barely conscious as we waited for a CT scan. The results only told us that his brain tumors were multiplying. I knew that. I could see small tufts of hair growing back, and to me that was bad news. If his hair was growing so were other things.

By Monday night he had declined significantly. He was in and out of consciousness. He had now been in the hospital four weeks. He thought he was crawling with spiders, he told us we smelled bad, he was seeing shadows; but in between he tried his best to be jovial old Dennis. I wanted to bring one of our dogs up to see him, thinking that would bring him some comfort, but he said they stunk too.

I wanted to simply lay down beside him and just hold him, but I wasn't allowed to even sit on his bed. He told me I was so fat that I would break the bed. If he had said that when he was healthy, he would have been dead a lot sooner!

Four weeks of hope. I find it fascinating now that I never, ever gave up hope. As if a miracle was just around the corner. When he was lying on his side, I would put the palm of my hand on his back and pray the tumors away. Every single day—I never gave up! I tried to get him to eat. "Please Dennis, just a mouthful," because that's what wives and mothers do, but I was told that the body refuses food as it prepares to shut down, and he had already stopped eating.

We never forgot the word we had picked together, that meant something to both of us. We hadn't shared it with anyone else. We said that word dozens of times a day until he could no longer talk, but I kept repeating it to him. That word was our secret code, our key to whatever lies beyond.

On Tuesday, June 27 we had a priest, well known to the family, come to give him the last rites. We had forgotten to discuss that aspect of his Catholic religion and now it was too late for him to address. We had discussed what he wanted at his funeral. He didn't want a full Catholic mass as he said it would be a waste of people's time. I asked if he wanted bagpipes played, and he said no because he wouldn't be there to enjoy them. It was a very strange and extremely difficult conversation.

The priest administered the last rites with our children, two nieces, his sister and brother-in-law in attendance. Afterward, I stepped into the hallway to thank the priest and say goodbye. That's when a very, very, strange thing happened, and it would be the first of many to come.

My brother-in-law Doug remained in the room with Dennis, who with great difficulty, began to speak. He asked where his cousin Clifford had gone. As explained to me later, this conversation took more than a few minutes because it was so difficult for Dennis to talk, but Dennis said that Clifford had just been there for a visit. Lovely, except Clifford had been dead for over a year. Dennis pointed to the wall where a cork bulletin board was posted and wanted to see the calendar. He tried to count the days on his fingers. He told Doug that Clifford said "something big" was going to happen on July 1.

## 28 – 11:52 p.m.

On Friday, June 30 I was told by a nurse that Dennis would die sometime during that day. A nurse or doctor could tell; I certainly couldn't.

Good friends of ours were there for a visit. They didn't know what I had just been told but they both knew that something wasn't right, and they decided to stay for me.

How do you prepare for this? What are you supposed to do? You wonder, how quickly is this going to happen? I've heard that often the person dying waits for loved ones to leave. I thought, should I leave and wait for a phone call? I just remember being in a panic and not having a clue what to do next. I began by picking up the phone and letting Dennis's family and best friends know. They were welcomed to join us, but I couldn't possibly give anyone an exact time.

I went home because I needed to hug our dogs. No one could comfort me but them. Thank heavens for a neighbor who had been taking care of them for the past month. When I came back to the hospital around one o'clock, I just sat there waiting for my husband to die.

There seems to be this rumor out there that death, and the passing from this life to the next, is a beautiful thing. It's not. All of it was ugly, the worst day of my life.

If Dennis had been trying to tell us that he would be leaving this earth on July 1, we had a long wait. Slowly over the afternoon friends and family arrived. I remember very, very little. I played music. Dennis loved, I mean really loved Celtic music. A friend in Ireland, upon learning of his illness, sent Dennis a CD by the Irish Tenors. Beautiful, beautiful music, so that is what I played.

By early evening we had a room full of people and slowly I began coaching Dennis to let go. I went back and forth from one side of his bed to the other, prompting, giving permission, and in the end pleading for him to let go and step over to the other side. I begged. I named names, his parents and family, friends, even Elvis who was waiting for him.

There was thunder and lightning outside. A huge storm orchestrated either for him or by him, but it was big, and he loved storms. Dennis fought like a beast, tooth and nail with every fiber of his being, but he would not let go.

There is no beauty in death. The only thing I do remember was hearing my son, at some point later in the evening say, "Where is Dr. Kevorkian when you need him?" This was torture for everyone in the room.

And the Irish Tenors sang on.

It was around 11:30 p.m. I heard our friend Bob, who had been there all day, burst from the room and run down the hall screaming for help. Dennis needed help. Put this man out of his misery! A nurse returned and gave him an injection and within minutes Dennis was quiet and he was gone. No movement, he was at peace and the raging storm outside stopped.

A nurse and doctor returned and pronounced him dead. It was Friday, June 30, 2000 and 11:52 p.m. How ironic that it would have been my parents' fifty-fifth wedding anniversary. They asked me if I wanted to stay awhile with Dennis as I understand some loved ones do. But this was not my Dennis. This was a shell, a broken baby bird. There was nothing left of the strong, broad-shouldered George Clooney lookalike man I had loved for thirty years. What remained could not cast a shadow.

Dennis had tried to tell us that something big was going to happen on July 1 and we didn't listen. That was his final request and we called for help too soon. We should have just sat there collecting our thoughts and saying a prayer before we called for him to be pronounced dead. Who would have known that it made a difference? Although the newspaper obituary read that he died on July 1, his death certificate reads June 30, 2000 at 11:52 p.m. Eight minutes short of what Dennis had told us and, I would soon learn, eight minutes short of one particular life insurance policy payout.

Splat!

# *Splat!*

"In the end what matters most is,
How well did you live, how well did you love,
and how well did you learn to let go."
—Buddha

## 29 – Moving Life Forward

I now had an entirely new life ahead of me. I wasn't going to tread softly into my future wearing dainty stilettos. No, I planned to attack as if I was in combat boots. This was a chance to start again. I could do and be anything I wanted, with no more responsibility.

Ha! That was a laugh and a half, when I couldn't even get out of bed. All I wanted was to lock the doors, pull down the shades and hide, perhaps forever. How could I possibly pick up where I left off six months ago? Everything had changed—absolutely everything—and instead of thinking big, which I usually did, all I could see from under the covers was my bleak future ahead.

I had an overwhelming feeling of failure because I was the one who held things together. I had always been the perfect daughter and found the perfect man to take over the family business. I'd been the best wife and mother I could be with no prior training for either of those jobs. Now I had no husband and our two children who were now grown up owned the family business. They no longer needed me in the way that they had. I had nothing to hold my life together and I felt completely out of control. All those things had given me purpose and now they had been taken away. My nest was truly empty. Yes, I had my own fashion business, but in those early moments the last thing I wanted to do was to motivate other women.

It was Saturday, July 8, the morning after the funeral, and I was alone. Dennis and I had done our "till death do us part" and now I was alone forever. If it was time to begin living again, I didn't have a clue where to start. How long could I hide from the world before someone noticed I was missing? I was afraid to take time to recover in case I never could. I knew that I had to keep going, so I decided I would put one foot in front of the other, every single day. "Don't stop," I said, "just keep on moving forward." I had to face my new world and my future even if I was doing it alone. Finally, on that Saturday morning, I got up, got dressed, and got into my car. I drove to Safeway and I bought all the ingredients I needed. I went home and made chicken soup for my soul. Though I felt utterly defeated, I knew that chicken soup could fix just about everything, even me.

The week of the funeral was a blur. My mom arrived, as did my cousin and two good friends from Toronto. My friend Carol and my mom would stay with me. I needed Carol to help me with my mom and get me through each day. It had been a very difficult six months in my relationship with my mom because of Dennis. With his intense dislike for her he made both our children promise that she would not be allowed in Winnipeg until after he died and was cremated. That was a tough one. Not that my mom could have been any help for me, but she loved her only son-in-law and although she wanted to be there for both of us, I had to respect my husband's last wishes and remind her that it was better to remember him as he was before he got sick.

I had taken six months to plan the funeral, write the eulogy and prepare a tribute. Night after night, once Dennis was asleep, I sat on our bedroom floor and sorted through our thousands of photographs to find ones that would tell the story of his life. Then I had them color copied so I didn't lose any. This was a process to keep my mind busy and to remind myself how handsome he was, because the Dennis I knew and loved had already slipped away. I bought six boards and rented six easels and arranged the photos to tell his story in decades. I hid everything under the bed so Dennis wouldn't find it. No one knew

Dennis better or loved him more, so I also felt the most qualified to speak about him. I could not measure the sadness or despair that week before the funeral, but I chose to remember the moments that brought a split second of joy or a smile to my face.

The night before the funeral we had another huge and violent storm just like the night Dennis left this earth. I don't like storms but for some unknown reason I didn't hear a thing. My friend Carol, who was sleeping down the hall, had to come in my room and close all the windows because of the loud thunder, while I didn't even know there was a storm. In fact, it was the best sleep I'd had in six months. Sadly, streets were flooded along with basements and many friends couldn't make it out of their homes that morning, so people I really hoped to see at the funeral weren't there.

I had paid a visit to my optician a few months earlier. I wanted to be sure that I would be able to see clearly when I delivered the eulogy. I was fitted with new contact lenses: one was for distance, because I wanted to see who was there, and the other eye was for reading up close which I would need if I glanced at my notes. As I was preparing for the funeral scheduled for 11 a.m. on Friday, July 7, I became totally hysterical because suddenly I could not see, not a single thing. The world was a blur. I was devastated and phoned my optician in a panic. She tried to calm me down and suggested that I remove the contacts I had inserted, throw them away and start with a fresh new pair. A minute later I phoned her back with an apology, laughing hysterically. Would you believe I had four contacts in my eyes? Yes, yet another "worst day of my life" had begun.

Music is important to me and I was quite specific about what music was to be played at the church. I flew my friend Arlene in from Alberta to sing one particular song that meant the world to me. It was one I hadn't heard in decades. Arlene recorded the song, then sang along with it while she played her guitar. It was Art Garfunkel's "All I Know," which he had recorded in 1973. If there was one song in my relationship with Dennis, that was it, and Arlene did a masterful job. There was another song by Barbra Streisand that was a favorite of mine. In order to hear it without breaking down, I played it for months every time I went through the car wash, where I screamed my lungs out to condition myself. Of course there were Dennis's favorites sung by the Irish Tenors, and the theme to the movie "Somewhere in Time," Rachmaninoff's *Rhapsody on a Theme of Paganini*. He loved that music.

After the ceremony the family left the church first and got into a limo that would take us to the hotel down the street for the reception. As we sat there, we could look up and see all our friends walking down the very steep and large set of church steps. All of a sudden, the limousine backfired, sounding like gunshot. Everyone on the steps jumped out of their skin. My children and I burst out laughing and said, "Dad did that!" No doubt about it.

Dennis was well known for pulling pranks. I mean he was BAD and would even cancel your hotel or flight reservations; but one day someone tried to get even, and it was the best trick of all time. It was back in May of 1980. Dennis was on a road trip and I was home alone in our first house with two children who were turning six and four. The phone rang just around suppertime. It was a news reporter from the *Winnipeg Tribune* and she asked to interview me because I was giving my home away for free. You have got to be kidding, I told her. Or failing that, she must have the wrong person. She asked if I subscribed to the *Winnipeg Free Press* and directed me to the classified section where I found the following advertisement:

"ATTENTION REFUGEES & IMMIGRANTS. We have a beautiful home with 5 bedrooms that we will volunteer for you to live in until you get settled in Winnipeg. No need to worry about rental rates its free! Please call Dennis or Adelle at 888-8534."

I could feel my knees buckle and I landed on the floor. Can you even imagine the thoughts that raced through my head? This was a time in history when many, many immigrants were arriving in Canada and needed homes. With Dennis out of town, could he be leaving us and giving away our house? This was before cell phones, so I didn't even have a way of tracking down my husband. Once I read the ad a few times I noted that my name had been spelled wrong and we didn't have five bedrooms. So maybe someone was messing with us. I phoned my neighbors to see if anyone could shed some light on this horrible situation, because I was alone with my two children and I was getting frightened. One neighbor suggested I alert the local police. They assured me they would cruise through the neighborhood more frequently that night. I was terrified of vans full of people landing in my driveway, as anyone, knowing our name, could look up our address in the phone book.

The next day I phoned the *Free Press* and requested that the ad be canceled. It was then I learned it was to run for three days! Within the hour the manager of the classified department phoned me, sounding rather shaken and pretty upset, but he gave me an explanation. Recently a couple were in the newspaper's front office wanting to place an ad for a home they were giving away. One of the staff felt that the request seemed suspicious and asked them to meet with the manager. The gentleman remained behind, but the female went to the manager's office to discuss the ad. He told me she introduced herself as Adele. She was very attractive, well put together and charming. He didn't even feel the need to ask for identification. He added that she was very professional and sincere. She went on to explain that she and her husband were most fortunate and wanted to share their good fortune with others by giving a home for free to someone who needed it. At his suggestion they phoned the local refugee center, but the lines were busy each time. Not a problem, she still wanted to place the ad.

The advertising manager apologized profusely, but luckily I didn't get one call or person ringing my doorbell. When Dennis finally arrived back home, he didn't have a clue about the ad and was just as stunned as me. Four months later I did get a call and only that one. It was a United Church minister who had heard the story at a party and couldn't remember if it was true or not. His church was sponsoring a family who needed a home and wanted to know if ours was available. Most of our friends confessed they weren't smart enough to come up with such a plan! Forty years later I still carry a laminated copy of the ad in my wallet. I've found it to be a great conversation starter, and some days I read it just to put a simple smile on my face.

In the eulogy I told many "Dennis" stories including that one about the newspaper ad from 1980. Later at the reception following the service, two of my friends, Edie and Lorie, approached me. Lorie looked wide-eyed and pale as she handed me an envelope. Inside was a sympathy card that she asked me to read. Her partner, who could not be at the funeral, owned a large and well-known fishing lodge in Canada's Arctic and was one of Dennis's best friends. In the card was a written confession that he had dictated to Lorie over the phone from the Arctic the evening before. He and Lorie and two other friends had initiated the newspaper joke on us. Now that Dennis was dead, and closer to the "powers that be," our "friend" felt it necessary to come clean. Simply because Dennis could now cause the fish stocks to dry up, create bad weather or cause fishing boats to sink, the truth now needed to come out. Confession is good for the soul. But thinking it was long since forgotten, they had absolutely no idea that I would bring the subject up twenty years later in the eulogy. On a day that was so terrible, their confession gave me a huge giggle.

At the reception at a local hotel following the service, I realized I had ordered far too much food. Obviously I was not in my right mind when I met with the caterer. Both my children delivered much of the excess to a downtown shelter, and the rest we saved for a party. Yes, we had a party, an Irish wake at an Irish pub. There are so many people you want to see and talk to and thank at a funeral but so little time, so my son and daughter made arrangements for us to have a large room for ourselves. Everyone was invited including all of our staff. When my son walked in, the bartender asked what kind of beer Dennis drank. That would be Sleeman's Honey Brown, so the bartender opened a bottle and put it on the bar in case Dennis showed up.

Dennis was very proud of his Irish heritage and we had planned to tour Ireland that month. The fashion company I worked for had a really fabulous Kelly green as one of their fall colors. I bought the entire collection for the trip that never happened. Instead, I proudly wore it to the Irish wake and put it in a charity box the next day. Ireland would have to remain just a dream.

## 30 – And So it Began

When Dennis and I first chose "the word" that meant something special to both of us, did I believe he could send me that sign from the grave beyond? Absolutely not. I really was simply dreaming that it could happen. I wanted to believe, but I knew it was less than likely. I let Dennis pick the word because I had learned he was to make all the decisions once he was terminal. He chose the word "Firebird" and it was not about anything with wings. It was about the Pontiac Firebird. Dennis owned one in the late '60s which he drove on our first date and which impressed the hell out of me. But, in order to pay for his divorce, he had to sell it, and for the next few years we drove a Chevy Vega station wagon. That's quite a reality check.

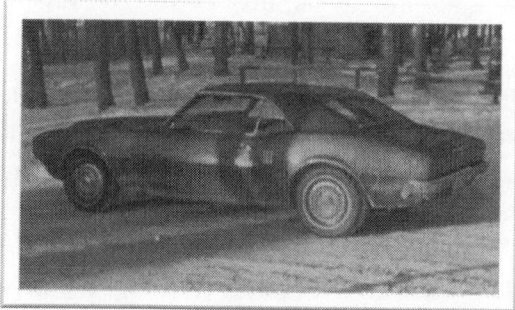

Dennis always dreamed of buying another Firebird, and since he did the car shopping without my input, I never knew what was coming. My neighbor had just bought a Ford Granada and I was oh so envious. It was silver with burgundy interior, four doors and a very large trunk. I wanted one badly, but what did Dennis buy me? A brand-new 1979 Pontiac Trans-Am Firebird, with a T-bar roof. Bronze in color with two doors, bucket seats and absolutely no trunk space. Our son was a goalie and I couldn't even get a hockey stick inside the car. Where on earth can you fit a hockey bag? It was a typical midlife crisis car for a man. I was not happy with my new wheels, but you can bet that I was the "hottest" housewife and momma on the road in 1979. I looked so good on my birthday that year that when I was stopped by the police for speeding, and I really was speeding, I talked my way out of a ticket.

That beautiful slick and shiny sports car had a tragic end. Around 1981 when it had hardly been broken in, Dennis had an accident. It was the beginning of April and melted snow and ice on the roads can freeze late at night. Dennis skidded though an icy patch at a stop sign and ended up on someone's front lawn, taking out their white picket fence. An off-duty police officer stopped to see if he was okay and learned very quickly that he had been drinking. The car was totaled and towed, and Dennis lost his license for a year. One of life's "I should have known better" lessons.

Now it was early July of 2000. Dennis was gone and I silently prayed that he, in some way, would send me "the word." Wouldn't that be cool? I started looking for a Pontiac Firebird to take my parking space, cut me off or speed past me. That car in any form would have made me a believer, but a message from the other side wasn't going to be that obvious, and I missed the very real reference to a Firebird for many years. When I did see the first sign from above, I saw it as simply a coincidence, nothing more, and I moved on.

The first strange thing that I can't explain happened two weeks after Dennis died, and one week after his funeral. It was a Friday night and my friend Shirley, and I went to a football game. It was my first time out in a long time and being in a large crowd with the opportunity to cheer and be happy was ideal. Then the weirdest thing happened. I looked to my right in the next section of the stadium, and about five rows in front of me was a man who, from the back, looked exactly like Dennis. In fact, he was wearing the same shirt Dennis owned. Funny, I thought, isn't that a coincidence. A few minutes later I looked and the man was gone. I wished that I had pointed him out to my friend, because this man never came back to his seat even though the game had just started. The moment made me smile, because Dennis really hated going to football games with me, so to have a man with thick silver hair wearing the same shirt Dennis had was really kind of funny. Or was it?

Many months later, when I was thinking about that evening, I started to question what I had seen. The man did have hair exactly the same color and style as Dennis, and there was no doubt that from behind he looked exactly like Dennis—but that was no ordinary shirt. I gave it to Dennis for Father's Day around 1990. Not an inexpensive shirt, it was really good quality, short-sleeved, and had drawings of fly fishing and lures all over it. I fell in love with it in the store, but Dennis said it was the ugliest shirt he'd ever seen. However, being the wise

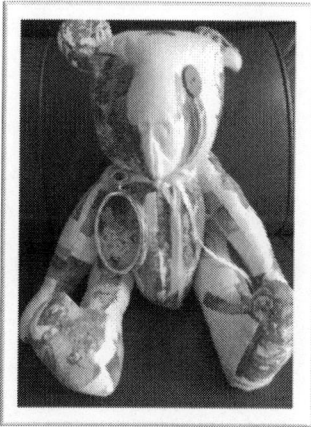

man that he was, and because it was a gift from me, he wore it, but only when we were out of town. I have a picture from almost every winter vacation with him wearing that shirt. He wore it where he wouldn't run into anyone who knew him. After he was gone, I sent it away, along with some other shirts, to a woman in the USA who was going to make them into teddy bears that I could give to the closest people in his life. Dennis always wore long-sleeved plaid shirts and I had many to use for bears. One went to each of our children, his best friend, Ron, his sister, Mary-Jane, and I think even his office manager got one as well as me. Each bear was to have big blue eyes just like Dennis. My bear still sits in my office today.

Why would this particular man, who was at the football game, go to his closet and pick out a fishing-themed shirt which was at least ten years old and wear it that night to a game? And, why in the presence of 26,000 people, would he just happen to sit in front of me? Then, once I saw him, he disappeared. The strings were being pulled. "Spooky shit" had begun to happen and to such a degree that over time, my girlfriends named me Witchy Woman.

## 31 – Pack Your Bags

In the year 2000 I would make nine different trips away from home that would take me to twelve different countries. I simply didn't want to sit still, or I would start thinking just how sad I really was. Even before Dennis left this earth, I had commitments over the summer months. I made a big mistake in the beginning because I thought I was doing just fine and could plan everything on my own. Not so. I was really a total mess. I needed help but of course would never ask.

One month after Dennis's death I flew down east for a week of R & R followed by a conference in Toronto. I booked a spa retreat near Toronto by picking a random name without even looking at a map to see where I was going. I thought the spa I had booked was in Niagara on the Lake, not too far from Niagara Falls. I failed to make arrangements to get there from the Toronto airport. Apparently, the only shuttle bus left in the late afternoon, so I had to sit at the Toronto airport and entertain myself for about five hours, which was longer than my flight there. When I finally arrived at the spa it was nowhere near the town I was aiming for. It took a $40 cab ride to get there and another $40 cab ride to get to Niagara Falls. This spa/hotel was off a major freeway and turned out to be a destination for tennis players, which I am not. There wasn't even a place where I could go for a nice walk. I was miserable.

This week would be full of "firsts." So, I went to the bar until my room was ready, ordered a glass of wine and sat all by myself. Without warning the sound system began to play Nat King Cole singing, "Smile though your heart is breaking." I lost it!

That night it was dinner alone, so tough for me to do. I took my room key and some tissues in case I began to cry again. I didn't take my purse, since if I was sitting by myself, I would want to look busy and I would systematically clean out my purse, because that's what women do. Back in my room, I turned the TV on to the movie channel to see what I could find to entertain myself. The movie I kept going back to was *American Beauty*. I'd seen it when the movie came out in 1999, knew that it had a tragic and terribly sad ending, but I couldn't stop myself from picking it. Kevin Spacey plays a character named Lester Burnham, a forty-two-year-old advertising executive who has a midlife crisis. As the movie comes to an end Lester is shot and killed. As his soul leaves this earth and his life passes before him, he tells the audience about one of his vivid memories: "The first time I saw my cousin Tony's brand-new Firebird." His character could have said Camaro or Ford Mustang, but he didn't. There was the word I'd been waiting for. But it would be almost ten years before I watched that movie again and realized that I was drawn to the movie because it held the "firebird" message for me.

The rest of the week went quite well. I did take that long taxi ride so I could do some shopping. I had also decided that I would build my summer cottage on the property Dennis and I had purchased for our twenty-fifth wedding anniversary. The décor would be French country blue and yellow, so on this trip I started shopping. To me it was a form of therapy—"retail therapy." I was making plans for my future and trying to move myself forward very slowly. Much better than talking to a therapist, crying my eyes out, writing her a cheque, then trying to compose myself enough to drive home again.

The week had one more big surprise for me. On my flight home I sat in business class and chatted with a lovely gentleman who sat beside me. Grief doesn't give you an advance warning. You never, ever know when it's going to strike. When the captain announced that we should prepare for landing, my mind went immediately to a scene I had repeated dozens of times before. I would deplane and begin looking for a man with silver hair as I descended the escalator to the arrivals area, because Dennis would always be there to pick me up. But not today, not ever again. As that realization reached out and grabbed me in a choke hold, as only grief can do, I snapped. That poor man beside me didn't know what had happened and I couldn't talk or explain. I was in a full-scale, snot-blowing, ugly cry and it wasn't about to be over soon.

Once I was back home, I got very busy very fast. Dennis and I had wanted to do a major renovation to our townhouse before he got sick, so the Monday after his funeral I met with a contractor. I planned to gut and redo the master bathroom and the kitchen. My contractor was a lovely man who, it turns out, had recently lost his wife. By the time we were upstairs making plans for the bathroom he began to tell me his story, and there we stood, tears streaming down our faces. He was the perfect person to do the reno because he knew what I was going though firsthand. Although just about everyone has horror stories about renovations, mine went smoothly; and having lots of people around, even if they were strangers, was a really good thing for me to do.

In the preparation for my reno I checked all areas of the house to see what else needed to be done. I found handwritten notes posted from Dennis in every little corner, reminding me when to turn the water off outside, or how often to have the furnace cleaned, or what I might need to do with the electrical panel if the power went out. Dennis could be very considerate and knew I would need some help. He also left three small cassette tapes carefully labeled with my name, Damien's, and Keele's. I didn't have the courage in that moment to listen, as it would be too painful and too soon to hear my husband's voice. It would take me almost two years before I could sit down and listen to them. They turned out to be blank, which was even more difficult to deal with. Either Dennis forgot to make the recordings, or he did and pressed the wrong buttons. By that point all I wanted was to hear his voice.

There was a very positive outcome from a decision Dennis had made when he knew he was dying. He chose the Rainbow Society for donations made in his remembrance after his death. The Rainbow Society helps fulfill the wishes of Manitoba children suffering from a life-threatening illness. In the beginning their office sent me a letter in response to a donation. Soon donations were so plentiful that they asked me if they could fax me the names. Those faxes came in by the dozens and were overwhelming, so they put all the names on one list instead of individual faxes, and reading those long lists became a daily event for me. Months later I received a beautiful letter from the

Rainbow Society thanking me. Never had any one person's request resulted in so much money donated. They were able to send an entire family to Florida for a vacation. Their little girl was blind and needed heart surgery and, thanks to Dennis, she was able to have her wishes come true at Disney World.

## 32 – Spooky Shit

Spooky shit, what else can I call it? There's no other phrase that works. Things happen continually that I cannot explain. I don't believe they were simply random, and they weren't a fluke because there were too many. Nothing quite like this had ever happened to me. When these strange things began to happen after Dennis died, and continued for many, many years, I came to believe that he was reaching out to say he was sorry, to give me guidance from afar, and just let me know he was keeping an eye on me. It was extremely comforting.

Having lived in rented apartments for years, my son wanted to purchase a house for himself, and Dennis had left him money to do so. Real estate was doing extremely well that summer, and every house Damien wanted me to look at with him was sold before we could see it. Finally, near the end of August, two months after his dad had died, Damien found his perfect house to look at. The street it was on was under construction and closed to traffic so no one else could see the For Sale sign. The minute we walked in, I didn't even have to go past the front hall. "This is your house," I said excitedly. It absolutely felt like he was supposed to be there. Offer submitted, offer accepted, a new beginning.

Then it began to strike both Damien and me that this was no ordinary house. In a city of well over 600,000, our family business was at the top of the same street, and although it always seemed strange to me, at the end of each and every workday, Dennis drove past the house that Damien had just purchased. During the years I worked in the business I drove home a completely different way. Dennis and I would get into our separate cars, take off in different directions and meet at home. Every day between 5 and 6 p.m. from 1974 to 2000, Dennis made a right turn in front of the home Damien had just purchased. To top that off, Dennis grew up a few streets away at 726 Sherburn, and Damien's new home was at 627 Spruce. The numbers were reversed. We like to think that Damien's dad picked the house for him.

Back in the '80s and early '90s Dennis dreamed of someday owning a Rolex watch. I had no idea why, but in 1997 when we were on a trip to Hong Kong, I had the opportunity to purchase one for him. He was most appreciative but felt it was too extravagant and said he would rather get two really good and very different Seiko watches instead, so that's what we did. When he learned that he was terminal he gave me specific instructions as to what I was to do with those watches when he was gone. The bulky stainless steel one with all the dials was to go to our daughter Keele's fiancé, whenever she found one. The gold, thin dressy Seiko was to be given to our son Damien when he got engaged. I could tell this was extremely important to him, but at this point neither of our children were even thinking about marriage.

Dennis passed on June 30 and a few days later I went into our safe to retrieve both watches. They weren't there. I checked the dresser, checked the closet, checked the entire house—no watches. I checked his office and boardroom at the shop, tore his truck and my car apart, even asked his sister to look through her house. No watches. Every pocket in every item of clothing he owned, no watches. At first, I simply thought I was still in shock, so should give it some more time, but I had to find those watches.

Towards the end of September my dear friend Paulette came from Victoria for a visit and we met for lunch. I told her that I believed in sending requests for help up to the universe, so I told her the story of the missing keepsakes. When I got home, I noticed that the message light on my kitchen phone was blinking. I played the message and couldn't believe what I heard. It was the Time Center at Polo Park. Apparently Dennis had brought two watches in for cleaning back in March and never returned for them. They called a courier for me and within thirty minutes those precious watches were in my hand. Talk about timing!

A month later I invited Ron and his wife, Delphine, for Saturday night dinner. Dennis and Ron had been best friends for thirty years and I knew it was going to be a very difficult evening. When they arrived, Ron told me that he didn't even want to get out of the car because it was so painful to be at what was now my home and not Dennis's. I had arranged the dinner so that I could give Ron one of the teddy bears I had made out of Dennis's old shirts, and he was very grateful. I don't remember what I served for the main meal, but I won't forget dessert.

I had found a recipe for a pear crumble that I wanted to try. That morning I was off to Super Store for just three things. Envelopes, a lime, and a package of something I'd never heard of before, amaretti cookies. Of course, I didn't write them down. Surely, I could remember three things.

I had to find someone in the stationery department to help me with the envelopes, but they didn't have the size I needed, and I guess that distracted me. I did have the lime in my hand but suddenly I couldn't remember what the third thing was. Clueless, I just stood there wracking my brain until I finally gave up and walked over with my lime to the cashier. I would have to go home find out what I was missing and come back again. Super Store is one of the largest grocery store chains in Canada, which is why it's called The Great Canadian Super Store. On a Saturday morning it's always very busy and at least fourteen checkout lanes were open. I didn't have to stand in line very long, but as we all do I looked at the trashy tabloids, and the packages of candy, chocolate bars and gum. There, on top of all the candy, was a plastic container, unopened, with a big label on the top that said Amaretti cookies. I was so shaken that I explained to the cashier what had just happened, and we just stood there staring at the box of cookies.

A month later my daughter and I flew to Toronto for a wedding. The gift we had purchased was a large set of kitchen knives in a wooden butcher block. This was still the year 2000, so airline security was very different than today. We packed the gift-wrapped knives in my red carry-on suitcase. The gift-wrapped knives filled up most of the suitcase and because we didn't want it to shift in transport and rip the paper, we packed our PJ's and underwear tightly around the edges. This was also a time before phones talked and played music. My daughter was listening to my Sony Walkman on the flight when the batteries began to fade. She asked if I had any new batteries with me, and of course I didn't, but I suggested that when we got to the Royal York Hotel, the smoke shop on the main floor just might sell them. Finally, in our room we put the carry-on bag on the bed and opened it so we could remove the wedding gift. There on top of the of the wrapped gift was an unopened package of AAA batteries. Spooky, right?

Every February the fashion company I was with had their annual conference in Toronto, and I went every year. At the Saturday night banquet and awards ceremony, the company president always wore a gown to die for. She looked like a princess every single year. But instead of putting the gown in a closet forever and never wearing it again, tickets were sold for it. Proceeds went to the Breast Cancer Institute, our company's preferred charity.

A year after Dennis died, and fully aware of the spooky things that had been happening to me, my dear friend Jeannette and I were having lunch at noon on the Saturday of the conference with two other gals. Jeannette announced that she really wanted to win this year's dress and had bought a single ticket, because all you needed was one ticket to win. Approximately 2000 tickets were sold each year, so with her odds were 1/2000. Because Dennis really loved her, I thought she needed a little help from above. Truly as a joke, I lifted my hands to the heavens while we were gathered around the restaurant table and said, "Dennis, you heard that Jeannette really wants to win that dress! See what you can do!"

After the banquet and awards that evening most of us didn't want to stay for the dance, and everyone on my team headed back to my room to party. Even I had little faith that Jeannette would win, but shortly after we settled in my room the phone rang and Jeannette was screaming from the ballroom that her ticket had been drawn and the dress was now hers. Gobsmacked! I was absolutely thrilled that Jeannette was the winner, but also felt a wee bit guilty that I didn't have any faith in the powers that be, and I wasn't there to watch her win and share the excitement of the moment.

Now you might think these things are random and simply a coincidence. Many of these times I asked a question and got an answer almost immediately. It didn't, however, work for every question or request I asked for. It's been almost twenty years and although I constantly ask, beg or plea, I am still waiting for winning lottery numbers.

It was around this time I picked up a book by Squire Rushnell called *God Winks*. It confirmed what I suspected, that these events, my "spooky things," were not a coincidence. Whether it was Dennis or a higher power, someone was keeping an eye on me; and each time something spooky happened, it was a message to me that I was on the right track and going in the right direction. This was only the beginning, because things began to happen by the truckload. Not a dump truck, fire truck or tow truck. It was a pickup truck, a Ford F150 that just happened to be burgundy.

## 33 – Truckload

In November of 2000 while sorting through Dennis's home office I found a picture of him I had never seen before. It was a Polaroid photo of him at the car dealership our friends owned. He was posing in front of his new burgundy F150 which was a 1998 model, I think.

That truck meant more to Dennis than any vehicle he'd ever owned, much to my annoyance. It was just a truck, but I had to take my shoes off when I got inside and wasn't allowed to cross my legs in the front seat in case my foot touched the dashboard. This wasn't even a luxury model, but it was Dennis's pride and joy. He was really a pain about it and took it to the car wash every Sunday to hand wash it and keep it looking like new. When he died it was given to our son. The day I found the photo I decided to have it framed professionally and that's when things started to happen. Yes, spooky shit by the truckload.

Here are a few of the incidents that really stood out to me:

The first time I noticed something different came a few weeks later, on a normal weekday evening in November. I went over to a friend's place for coffee and took my two dogs with me. On the way home I had to stop at a red light at the top of their street. When the light turned green, I was the only one sitting there, but something made me pause. Normally I would have put my foot on the gas and moved forward and into a left turn. But there was a whisper in my head that said, "Don't move." I paused for about five seconds, and in that short amount of time a giant semi-trailer ran the red light at full speed. If I had not held back for those few seconds my puppies and I would have been nothing but a splat on the road. I slowly turned left, then right onto Surgeon Creek Road, and that's when I noticed a burgundy F150 behind me. I was a little shaken and, in the moment, didn't think anything of it. A few minutes later I looked in the rearview mirror again and realized the burgundy truck was following me home, up close, and right to my driveway.

In early May of 2002, my daughter and I were stopped in front of the family business when the office manager ran out to my car with a panicked look on her face. Even though this was the month of May, we'd had a fluke snowstorm that morning. I didn't know until that moment that Damien had been in an accident and was in the hospital. He was driving his dad's truck to the US border to pay a call on our customs broker. The drive is only about seventy miles so it's usually an easy one, except in a blinding snowstorm. Damien didn't realize that he was actually driving in the ditch at one point because there was zero visibility. There was a side road with a culvert which by now was covered by snow and totally invisible. There's only one way to describe what happened: he did a "Dukes of Hazard" up and over the culvert, flying through the air and landing hard enough on the other side to bend the frame of the 5000-pound truck!

What a "coincidence" that an off-duty paramedic was following him in her car. After seeing what happened, she called 911 and plowed through the snow to see how badly he was injured. I didn't have a cell phone back then so no one could reach me. Apparently, the hospital was releasing him, and I went straight to his house just as he was arriving home. At the time the hospital released him it was not believed that he had suffered any serious injuries, and fortunately he hadn't; though once he was home, the hospital phoned to say that he did crack a lower vertebra. How lucky was my son to have not been seriously injured or stranded alone in a ditch? What would have happened if someone hadn't been in the right place at the right time to offer help? All these years later, he's never experienced any back trouble since the accident.

A few months later, I was in Calgary and spent the day with my friend Debbie. She too has experienced more than her share of spooky things, so she understood when we encountered constant sightings of Ford F150s that day. She and her husband also knew Dennis. I know it's said that when you buy a red car suddenly you realize that everyone in the world is driving a red car, but my experiences were much different, at least up until that day driving around Calgary. We were both with the same fashion company and we had to make a few deliveries to some of her customers. Those darn burgundy trucks were everywhere. We couldn't stop laughing and joking that Dennis knew we were together. The last place we stopped was in a small cul-de-sac. When we turned her car around there was a burgundy F150 right in front of us, as if it was staring us down. There were no other vehicles in sight.

The next month my friend Robin's mother passed away in Regina, Saskatchewan and my friends Penni and Gord came with me to the funeral. It's at least a six-hour drive and we had no time to spare coming or going. They had heard of my crazy truck "sightings" but I'm sure they didn't take me seriously until that day. From the funeral home in Saskatchewan to the Manitoba border we were literally stalked by a burgundy F150. It was not back a couple of hundred yards but right on my tail. Just as we hit the border it turned south, and we waved goodbye.

In February of 2003 I was in Quebec City on a company trip that included the Winter Carnival. Quite a group of us were leaving to fly home at the same time so we were bussed out to the airport. The first leg of the trip would be to Toronto, but we had mechanical problems even before we boarded our flight. The weather wasn't good, and the parts needed for the plane had to come from Toronto. It would be a long wait. It was not a large aircraft and several couples felt uneasy about what we were experiencing. They decided to stay another night and rebooked for the next morning. I had no problem with taking the flight. I watched the mechanics drive out to the runway where the airplane was stopped. They were in, you guessed it, a burgundy F150. I knew I would be safe.

In June of that year I was back in Toronto for another company meeting. On our second evening my friend Julie and I took a taxi to a nearby restaurant, where I shared some of my F150 encounters. After dinner, it was so beautiful out that we decided to walk back to the hotel. We expected to find a sidewalk or easy path to follow but we were on the edge of a ditch beside a freeway. The ditch was full of broken bottles, cans and garbage—not a very safe place to walk. When we got to the exit ramp we couldn't walk across the road. We just stood there for about fifteen minutes watching everyone whiz past us; no one would stop. Finally, someone did stop to give us the break we needed, and we ran across the road as quickly as we could. I looked back and was astonished to see that it was a burgundy F150, which in that moment seemed out of place. This was Toronto, the big city, not the Western prairie. People drive trucks on the prairies and Mercedes sedans in Toronto. I said to Julie, "Look, it's another truck!" Julie's response was, "Oh my God, I should have looked to see Dennis," and I said, "Dennis doesn't drive the trucks, he just sends them." We laughed like crazy.

October 16, 2003 was a Friday and I was driving to a meeting in a downtown hotel. I had not been in this particular parking garage before and was a bit lost as to where I should be. Suddenly, I was cut off by a vehicle coming down the exit. I had to really slam on my brakes. It was, of course, a burgundy F150. I was not only stopped in my tracks but a little shaken that we had missed colliding by only inches.

When I found a new parking spot, still wondering where I was supposed to be going, I had a thought that I should be mindful of my surroundings. I always saw a sighting of an F150 as a gentle reminder, and this time it felt more violent. I walked through a door in the parking lot that I thought must be the way to the hotel. Once inside, I could see that there was another door a few stairs down leading into a hallway. "Perhaps there's an elevator at the end of the hall," I thought. I was wearing a skirt that was mid-calf length and a low pair of heels. I put my left hand on the stair rail and had my briefcase in my right hand. The last thing I remember was the sensation that my cheek bones were being shoved into my eye sockets. A hotel maid found me on the second floor of the hotel with ripped stockings, bloody knees and a cut lip, and I have no recollection of how I got there.

My friends cleaned me up and I sat through the meeting and drove myself home. I hurt everywhere. I went to bed with some bags of ice for my face and knees and went to sleep early. The next morning, I could barely get out of bed, but I had a plane to catch. I had skinned both knees and split my lip, but this morning they weren't too bad. I was in pain all over. I was flying to Vancouver where I would meet my mom and take the next plane to Las Vegas. We had seventh row seats to see Celine Dion at Caesar's Palace, and no matter how bad I felt, I could not cancel.

As the plane sat on the runway waiting to take off, I looked out the window. Positioned on the side of the runway was a burgundy F150. Of course, one would show up to let me know I would be okay. By Monday my face was black and blue but could be covered with makeup. Once back home I went straight to the doctor for X-rays and then to my chiropractor. The X-rays showed no fractures, but my chiropractor suggested I go back to the place I fell to see what caused it. He told me my neck and shoulders were so out of alignment that it was almost as if I'd hit the dashboard of a car. I went back to the parking garage. The second door I had walked through had a sign that said, "This door must be closed and locked at all times." Well it wasn't closed the day I fell. At the top of the three stairs I could see the rebar was raised above the cement steps which had sunk. It appears my heels caught on the rebar, catapulting me down the stairs and onto my face. How I didn't break my nose or knock out my teeth is a mystery to me. Even though I was wearing sunglasses that day, they didn't even have a scratch.

Someone was looking out for my welfare that day for sure.

## 34 – Angels Are with Me

There are five stages in the process of grief and recovery. They are: 1. Denial and isolation, 2. Anger, 3. Bargaining, 4. Depression, 5. Acceptance. People who are grieving do not necessarily go through the stages in the same order or experience every one of them. I don't remember going through five different feelings because I got stuck in anger right from the beginning and I couldn't move on from there. I was pissed at Dennis. Really, really pissed. How could he—how dare he—leave me, disappear and vanish forever just after we had found our perfect place? He was strong and healing, I was healthy, and he left me. He didn't leave us, he just left me. That's what it felt like; it was all about me and I needed help desperately. I'd only been angry a few times in my life, for very short periods, and I got over it quickly. This I was not getting over.

I have several friends who had been in a recovery program, a destination workshop, and I decided I needed to do this. You could be recovering from any number of things that were upsetting your life—an eating disorder, a loss, your childhood, absolutely anything. I felt it would be faster and easier than being in a group program that met once a week, or seeing a therapist. My biggest fault in life is that I am not a very patient person, so it was more like, "Fix me, and fix me fast!" No one asked and I told no one what I'd been going through. So, in the summer of 2002 I went on an eight-day adventure to heal myself. The most amazing things happened while I was there, and I wasn't alone.

I didn't think a person, a process or anything could help me. I was really at a breaking point. My friend Jeannette drove me to the airport so I wouldn't chicken out. I don't even remember the trip there or the first evening, but the very next morning before anything got started, I decided I was going to leave. I took a cup of coffee outside to the front steps of the building. Not to the patio and seating area where everyone else had gathered. I wanted to be alone. All by myself, and miserably alone, waiting for someone to rescue me and take me to the airport. I decided if a taxi pulled up, I would get in it and send for my clothes later. I just couldn't do this.

A taxi did pull up and a man got out with a small suitcase. He walked towards me, but I was so consumed with wanting to get out that I did not see the resemblance to Dennis at that time. I just stared at him and said, "You are in the right place." In that moment I had no idea what I meant or where that came from. I now think it was my soul speaking, because I would soon learn that I was in the right place and a life-altering experience was just moments away.

On the first morning we were assigned chairs, in a circle, and told we were to keep those chairs for the whole week. There were about twenty men and women of all ages from all parts of North America. We wore name tags but only knew each other's first names. The first morning we were given a verbal schedule as one of the facilitators turned the pages of a flip chart.

The word "addiction" appeared on the flip chart, and it was a real trigger for me. I leaned forward to see better but a man about six chairs away was blocking my view. I took one look at this man, burst into tears and ran from the room. His name was Andrew, and to me he looked exactly like Dennis did when he had lost his hair and was dying. Same height, weight, bald head, dressed like Dennis would have, and wearing the same glasses. I was completely freaked out and didn't understand why this was happening. After our first coffee break, and against the instructions we'd been given, Andrew was sitting beside me on my right and he would remain there the entire week. Each and every time we got paired with someone, I got paired with Andrew. We did virtually everything together and he stayed in that chair beside me the entire time.

The other man reminding me of Dennis, the one who had arrived while I waited on the front steps for someone to rescue me, was named Len. The physical resemblance to Dennis was uncanny, and I admit it disturbed me a lot. He was there, not as part of the process, but to learn how to be a facilitator. This meant he did not take part in anything and always remained outside the circle looking in. That was

Dennis. He never joined in anything in thirty years. No matter where we were, he always made me feel that he was anxious to leave.

I had brought along a photo of Dennis and me for that week (below, left); and on the second day I shared it with the group, including Len. Everyone was taken aback by just how much the two men looked alike. They could have been twins. However, I was recently in contact with the two other people who were in the original photo with Len (cropped version, below right). I had not been in contact with either one since 2003. They couldn't tell me who he was or where he'd come from, even though he was part of the programming that week. They couldn't help me at all. It was as if he never existed.

The photos of both men, Andrew and Len, were the reverse of Dennis, as Len has his hair parted on the other side and Andrew wore his watch on the opposite arm.

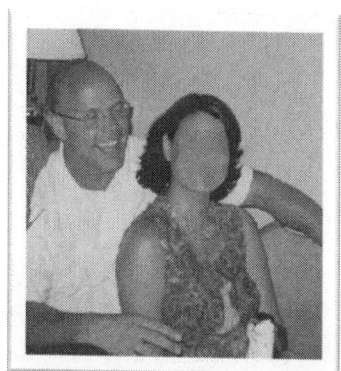

Once home I emailed everyone to see if anyone in the group had a photo of Andrew, and I was sent a picture. It just happens to be facing the reverse direction of one of the few photos of Dennis taken before he died. The picture of Dennis was taken on his fifty-fourth and last birthday. I cannot explain how having not one, but two men so similar to my husband, who was now dead, made me feel. It creeped me out a bit, but it was also very comforting. This was no coincidence. This was Dennis in both spirit and appearance supporting me and helping me to heal. I really believe that week, angels were with me.

There was one more thing about that week that I remember clearly. Almost every evening all the girls would get together, turn up the music and dance—just for fun and to let our hair down a bit. There was one song that was played every night. It was "Moon Dance," by Van Morrison, one of my all-time favorites. When that played, I would raise my arms up as if I was dancing with a man and I would waltz around the room. Yes, they made fun of me but night after night I didn't care and told the group that when the man for me showed up, "Moon Dance" would be playing.

## 35 – This Too Shall Pass

Our bodies and minds go through tremendous stress when we lose a loved one. It's a shock to the system that many ignore. Over the past two decades I have really been an advocate for anyone who has suffered the loss of a loved one, to keep a close check on their own health. I can't count how many friends and acquaintances I know who suffered from cancer within a short time after their spouse's or child's passing. I didn't. Even though I was a hot mess I still believed I was invincible. I think with the stress I had already lived through that if I had cancer in my genes, I would have had it by now. But, no, I would get something completely different.

The first thing the doctor discovered was that my thyroid was barely functioning. I'd been on medication since 1984, but I was topped up with a stronger dose and took off to Mexico with my eighty-two-year-old mother for a Christmas vacation. It was not fun and extremely difficult for me to function. Upon returning home I went to Montreal for a few days of business, but at the meetings I was constantly nauseous and had to leave the meeting room several times to lie down.

Back to the doctor for more tests. Results showed I was losing large amounts of protein through my urine. I saw a nephrologist or kidney specialist very quickly. Two biopsies were performed on my kidneys. I went to the hospital clinic by myself, certainly not expecting any bad news. I will never forget the look on the doctor's face and the expression in his eyes. It made the hair on the back of my neck stand up. I had a very rare and serious kidney disease called *Focal segmental glomerulosclerosis* (or FSGS). This disease, while rare, was the leading cause of kidney failure in adults.

Splat!

Still in shock, I had to get educated very fast. This "nephrotic syndrome" occurs when damage to the capillaries of the glomeruli causes proteins to leak into the urine. The simple explanation, which I clearly understood, was that the filters in our kidneys should look like window screens but mine were like fish-net stockings. There was no underlying cause identified. This was like one in a million. The very, very strange thing about this particular kidney disease is that it is more likely found in African American men than Caucasian women over fifty. Notable FSGS patients include Sean Elliott and Alonzo Mourning, both former NBA players; Clyde Simms, a retired pro soccer player; Andy Cole, former Manchester United football player; Aries Merritt, Olympic champion; and Flex Wheeler, a pro bodybuilder; as well as the late actor Gary Coleman and singer Natalie Cole. All are African American, and many had transplants. The only Caucasian person I found listed was Ed Hearn, a former baseball player for the New York Mets and Kansas City Royals, who also had a kidney transplant.

More tests and an immediate regime of prescription drugs followed, which included 120 ml of prednisone every other day. I swear that made me feel insane, and by 3 p.m. each day I was so wired, I had to take anti-anxiety medication to keep me from shaking uncontrollably. The best-case scenario, as explained to me, was to become prednisone-dependent for life, or be placed on a transplant list. I was also warned that with the large amount of steroids I was taking I could gain as much as a hundred pounds. Fuck!

I was so very, very alone in this battle, and a battle it truly was. I created a binder with all the information I could find on the disease. On the cover, I had a cartoon of people doing "the happy dance," and a title, "This Too Shall Pass." I was NOT going to allow this to take me down. No way in hell! I also decided to keep on living as if this wasn't even happening. I went to Italy in May for two weeks and Paris in the fall. The side effects weren't any fun, but I could not let them overwhelm me. My skin became so thin it was like parchment paper. I was afraid that my skin would tear. Even a walk wearing comfortable shoes produced bleeding blisters in a very short distance. I bruised constantly, and my face, which was now as big as the moon, was covered in lovely peach fuzz.

I beat this disease after a sixteen-month battle, and it has never returned. March is National Kidney Month, and from the mid-'80s to the mid-'90s, Dennis would buy a table or two at the Annual Kidney Foundation Dinner and invite his buddies in support of the charity. I asked him more than once why he supported a kidney charity, when every man in his family died from cancer. I remember him clearly telling me that people with kidney problems need our support too. Then after he passed, I got a rare kidney disease, and so did his best friend, Ron, who is on dialysis today.

When I was told that I might gain a hundred pounds, I figured I might as well enjoy the ride and didn't limit myself at all. I can gain five pounds just by reading a cookbook, but for the sixteen months I was on prednisone I didn't gain an ounce. There is no question in my mind that I conquered this kidney disease because I had an attitude and I had angels—and in the end, I was the one doing the happy dance.

## 36 – Dipping My Toe in the Water

In a few short years I had lived through my husband's addiction, my dad's suicide, two life-threatening illnesses, and my dear husband's terrible death to cancer. That's a lot, in fact more than enough for an entire lifetime. But it was about to get worse. Life would become more stressful, and even more heartbreaking, resulting in an ocean of tears for the next twelve years. Why? At the ripe old age of fifty-three I decided, with the encouragement of my son, to try internet dating. What was I thinking?

I had been a widow for three years, and I was on massive doses of steroids for my kidney disease, which gave me the huge prednisone moon-face. I couldn't have felt worse about myself if I tried. So why not step further out of my comfort zone? I thought that I couldn't possibly feel lower than I did at that point in my life, and yet it did get worse—over and over, and over.

How do you meet someone these days? I hadn't had a date since 1970 and didn't have a clue where to start. My son had quite a bit of luck on the internet so I decided that I would give it a try. I had already tested my bravery and replied to an ad in the personal columns in the paper. I was terribly nervous, my voice kept cracking on the recorded phone call, and I did not get a reply. I didn't have a clue that rejection would become a regular pattern in my life.

I don't even remember the first website I went on or if I wrote much about myself. I certainly wouldn't have posted a picture of myself with my moon face. But I will never forget my first date. We met at a coffee shop and had absolutely nothing to talk about. He was as nervous as I was. He was newly separated and hadn't dated much. There was no attraction, and I haven't got a clue what his name was. When my mom asked me later that evening how my first date went, I told her he got in his car and I could see that he was immediately on his cell phone. "Probably," I told her, "calling his wife to say he would pick up Chinese."

On my second date, at another coffee shop, I recognized my date as he was crossing the street and I felt the urge to hit the gas and run him down, but I didn't. Date #2 was even worse than date #1. I told him that if I was ever on life support my children weren't to pull the plug until I was down to a size four. His sarcastic reply: "When were you ever a size four?"

They say bad things come in threes, but date #3 was actually wonderful and exactly what I needed. Can't remember his name, either, but this single father of two young girls invited me out for martinis at the Fort Garry Hotel Piano Bar. I was thrilled! I got to dress up and use valet parking and even wore my mink coat, not thinking how that might intimidate him, me showing up like the queen. He was several years younger, very good looking and dressed very nicely. We had a fantastic time. I don't drink martinis and I was driving but I did have one glass of wine. When it was time to leave, my car was out front, and the valet referred to my date as my husband. That was the one split second that I felt almost sick to my stomach, because it was a reminder that I had no husband. He must have sensed that I was suddenly uncomfortable and in that exact moment, grabbed me in a big hug followed by a full-on kiss on the mouth. Damn, I needed that! My lips quivered for miles.

We met again the next morning when I picked him up at his home. I had my two dogs with me, and we went for a beautiful walk in the snow, on a morning filled with crisp air and sunshine. Later we stopped for coffee at Starbucks. It was all great and I was smiling from ear to ear. However, it came as no surprise that he called me mid-week to tell me we wouldn't be meeting again. He was actually a lot younger and wanted more children, and although he didn't say it when we met, he could see I was long past my "best before" date.

That was it for me. I'd put my toe in the dating pool and the temperature was not inviting. But my courage had been encouraged, and for some unknown reason I went nationwide. I joined another internet dating site and started looking for men in British Columbia, 1500 miles from Winnipeg. God only knows why. He really does.

## 37 – My Top 10 List

It's a fact that widowed or divorced women lose most of their couple friends. Sad but very true. One day shortly after Dennis passed, I walked through my dining room and realized that I would never entertain again. Dennis and I had done a lot of entertaining over the years.

In September 2000, when my renovations were finished, I had the strong urge to have friends for dinner to show off what I had done to the place. That's when I formed my infamous "Single Women's Gourmet Dinner Club." I invited three other single ladies who were between the ages of forty and fifty. Donna had never been married, Helen had lived through the divorce from hell, Jeannette had just left a twelve-year relationship, and I was the token widow. I've always been an organizer and instigator, and this would prove to be a perfect outlet for us all. I called our little club, "Sexless in the City," and the tongue-in-cheek goal was to get kicked out of the club. I won't tell you who went first.

The word "gourmet" was dropped almost instantly because the two women who had never been married went into panic mode whenever it was their turn to cook; things became quite casual rather quickly. At Christmas we did dress up for dinner at Helens, and for our entertainment she had invited a Tarot card reader to forecast our future. I'd been to one, years before, and had very low expectations.

On this particular first reading, in December of 2000, the Tarot card reader told me I would be moving. No surprise. It was common knowledge among my friends that I had planned to build a cottage at a golf course property called Grand Pines which was north of Winnipeg. Dennis and I had purchased it for our twenty-fifth anniversary. In my travels and in particular in the years to come I would purchase French blue and yellow household items for my imaginary cabin. By 2005 I would have collected everything but pots and pans. I also planned to move out of Winnipeg a year or two later. When my daughter Keele decided to move west with her boyfriend I decided I would purchase a condo there for my winters, pulling up stakes in Winnipeg entirely.

On this particular first reading, in December of 2000, the Tarot card reader told me I would be moving. No surprise. But then she said, "Don't you go to Alberta, you will never be happy there." That shocked me! She followed with, "You need to go somewhere green and hilly surrounded by water, like Vancouver Island." Well, I thought, that was a waste of $30. The capital city of British Columbia is Victoria, on Vancouver Island. It is known to be for "the newly wed and the nearly dead." Why on earth would I ever go there?

The beginning of the new year found me still on the internet searching. What else is there to do during the long nights of a Winnipeg winter? I was simply bored. The Tarot card reader had planted the seed and searching the West Coast of Canada for single men became an earnest undertaking. Though this would be my winter hobby I truly wasn't expecting to find much, if anything. Did I even know what I wanted? That required some heavy thought. I needed to narrow the parameters of what I wanted and needed in my life. You have to know what you want in order to find what you need, so I made "The List" and got ready to send it out to the universe. In no particular order:

1. A tall golfer with his own lunch money. I had dreamed of taking up golf in my fifties and I wasn't about to share my lunch money with anyone. Tall? I would soon learn that while women may tell a white lie about their age, men definitely lie about their height. Seems they were all six feet tall at some point.

2. I really preferred a widower. Someone who had been through a similar life experience. Losing your partner is a huge thing to have in common and it starts the conversation almost immediately.

3. I wanted to meet someone with a sense of fun and adventure. I wanted a gentleman who loved to travel. Extremely important. I loved my mom and girlfriends to bits but had traveled too much with the women in my life.

4.  The man for me would have to be able to show emotion and have empathy. He had to be able to open up and share his feelings on all subjects.

5.  I preferred someone who was an entrepreneur as opposed to a professional. I wouldn't have wanted a doctor, dentist or lawyer, just wouldn't.

6.  This man had to come clean-shaven or be willing to shave off his beard or mustache. I have never been attracted to facial hair.

7.  A strong appreciation for the arts would be a huge asset. I wasn't about to give up those interests. I had season tickets to the ballet and two live theatres.

8.  Dog lover was a necessity because I have two Bichons. Not too keen on cats as I am highly allergic to them.

9.  A sports fan was an absolute must. Particularly, he must be a football fan. When Dennis and I met, I just assumed that all men loved sports. Wrong. I was raised cheering on the home team, but Dennis wasn't interested at all. My son and I had season tickets to professional football starting in 1985 when he was turning ten. It became our "mother–son" thing. The Canadian football championship is called the Grey Cup, which is the equivalent to the American Super Bowl, and I have been to five different cities across the country for that final game in late November. I really mean the game, and not the partying that comes with it. When the Grey Cup came to Winnipeg in 1991 my son and I sat in -10 °F temperatures. That's how much I love the game.

10. Number 10 may sound weird, but the man of my dreams had to have hair. It's the fashion for balding men to shave their heads these days. Dennis had the most beautiful thick silver hair as his hair turned grey very prematurely. Those bald heads remind me of radiation and chemo and the battle Dennis encountered. I'd soon be surprised how difficult it was to find men with any hair at this age. Bald, they say, is beautiful, but not to me.

Was this written in stone? Of course not. You have to keep the list short and specific. It goes without saying that I wanted a family man who had a great sense of humor, who was polite and well-mannered, so those weren't listed. One thing I left out, not on purpose but because it never entered my mind. I should have added, or even had at the top of the list, "a man with class." Does that mean that the future would hold a lot of frog kissing? No! It would never get that far, because I would spend the bulk of my time turning over rocks.

## 38 – Geoff Smith

It was now mid-February 2004, and I was about to be dealt a big blow. One of my Bichons, Rocky, died with very little warning. Both he and his brother, Mozart, were getting older, having turned thirteen, and health issues were becoming apparent; but you're never, ever prepared for a death in the family, even when it is a family pet. These puppies were my life and had been by my side through all of life's stresses.

My son met me at the vet at seven thirty in the morning, and along with Rocky's big brother we said our goodbyes. I clung to Moe. It was now me and him against the world. Every night I scanned the internet for available men in British Columbia, scolding myself each time I did. Such a waste of my time.

Then one cold winter day in March I found something, or rather someone, interesting. Not one, but two men in BC caught my attention. I wrote both. One lived in Kelowna and the other in Victoria, on Vancouver Island. The strange thing about the one in Victoria was his photo. He had a full beard and had posed with a very large dog. I prefer clean-shaven men and I am definitely a small-dog person. I couldn't even fathom why I would take the time to write but felt compelled to do so. The chap in Kelowna challenged me to a phone call so I called him and pressed the delete button as soon as I hung up the phone. I could tell even in a brief conversation that he'd been drinking quite a bit. Absolutely not interested.

The other man, in Victoria, was recently separated and living temporarily with his sister. His name was Geoff Smith. By Monday morning we were connected via video camera so I could chat and see him, but there was no way I was willing to introduce my prednisone moon face to a stranger even if he was across the country. This became a regular thing. We would check in a few times a week and chat. He would be the first to say that I "glommed" on to him and I admit I did. I also put the blame on the massive amount of prednisone that I was still on for making me overly emotional. I couldn't shake the feeling that I was supposed to know him even if we had absolutely nothing in common. Geoff was a child-and-family therapist. He had a sympathetic and patient nature and I guess that was the attraction because that is exactly what I needed. It was just fun to have someone to talk to. What really grabbed my attention was his line of work. Geoff had worked in the area of addiction in Canada's North, and once he moved to Victoria, he worked at an addiction center. I felt that was no small coincidence. He was a Harley guy who loved to play the guitar, but not golf. He had been divorced or separated more than a few times and had one son. He wasn't anything on my list, but I still had this overwhelming need to know him. I would keep digging.

One morning I asked Geoff where he had traveled on his Harley, and he named dozens of places including the Red Lake Road. My wonderful Aunt Marj was from Cochenour, a small mining town in northwestern Ontario, and that's where I spent part of my childhood summers. I couldn't believe it! Few even know there is a Red Lake Road, let alone had been there. I thought that was an incredible coincidence. Too good to be true. His recently estranged wife was from there. I asked Geoff his wife's name, but it didn't ring any bells.

A month later I was off to Italy for a few weeks with my friend Linda and a great group of fellow travelers. It was the first time Linda and I had reconnected in twenty years. She was also from the town of Cochenour, and in fact that is where we met when we were about ten years old. I asked Linda if the name of Geoff's wife meant anything to her, and she didn't know of her either.

I don't even know at what point it hit me, but one evening once I was back home and settled in, I couldn't stop thinking about the fact that Geoff's wife was from Cochenour. That just made the world seem so small and a wee bit weird to me. It's a very small town and everyone knows everyone. Then as if I'd been stuck by lightning, I got it. I picked up the phone and called my cousin Bob (my Aunt Marj and Uncle Jim's son) and asked him if my suspicion was correct.

Once I was into my teens, I stopped flying north to visit Aunt Marj and Uncle Jim but did drive up there with my parents for their twenty-fifth wedding anniversary. At that time, I met a little girl in my aunt's kitchen. She was six and I was sixteen and her name was Michelle. To Marj, that little girl and I were the daughters she never had. She loved us both. Through the years, Marj talked to me about Michelle, as they became very close. In fact, when Marj passed away in 1991, I flew up to Cochenour for the funeral. Michelle, who couldn't attend, wrote a beautiful poem that was read at the funeral. I still have the copy of the poem with her name at the bottom. I would then discover that this same Michelle was Geoff Smith's soon-to-be ex-wife! What are the odds? I truly felt that somehow Aunt Marj had arranged this so Michelle and I could make a connection. She wanted "her girls" to be friends and Geoff Smith was the conduit. Years later I reached out to Michelle on social media and she flew in for a weekend visit. It was wonderful to get to know her and we will be connected forever.

I felt that there was still more to knowing Geoff, so by mid-June I suggested we meet in person when I was visiting Calgary and he was in Edmonton settling his personal life. My dog Moe and I drove to Canmore and Geoff drove south to meet me. I remember him getting off his Harley with my first impression being "John Wayne." To me he looked like a cowboy dismounting a horse. It was a very nice weekend, but I knew this man was not for me. He was lovely, kind and easy on the eyes, but we were complete opposites.

I was still on steroids and a mess from worry. I did not sleep for the most part of the weekend because I was constantly wired to the max. Geoff and I talked and talked the entire weekend—he on one couch and me other the other. Honestly it was very therapeutic. That's when I learned his story and I knew that it was very much the reason that I had reached out to him. Just like Dennis, Geoff had a son. It was an unplanned pregnancy from an early marriage that didn't work. And, just as with Dennis, his son's mother fought to get sole custody of their child. But Geoff fought back. He refused to give up this son, no matter what the circumstances. Today he and his son are extremely close, as he was always a part of his life. It brought to mind the question: what if Dennis had done the same? Rather than fight for his son, he allowed guilt and regret to rule his life.

## 39 – I See Dead People

When the movie "Sixth Sense" came out in August of 1999 and the line "I see dead people" became famous, I certainly didn't think that I would be one of those lucky people who could relate to it and chime in that I saw dead people too. That took until October 2003, and then I really did see dead people—or rather, just one person, Dennis.

I was trained by Dennis to keep a spotlessly clean car because he was obsessive about keeping all of our vehicles immaculate. After he was gone, I took my car to the Rainbow Car Wash weekly to hand wash it. It was around the end of October that I began to notice that even though there were only five or six bays for hand washing, there was always a burgundy F150 there. One day I struck up a conversation with the man beside me who was driving one. I told him all about my late husband and his favorite truck and asked if he was enjoying his. Each and every week a burgundy truck would be there, and eventually I went just to see if one would really show up. It became a game to me.

By the third week in November, I had a coffee date after supper, so I took my car to be cleaned around two thirty in the afternoon. I noticed out of the corner of my eye that once again there was an F150, and as I walked around the corner of my car, I looked up at the man drying his truck and I was frozen to the cement floor. The man was about Dennis's height and build, he had silver hair and was wearing what we used to call Dennis's uniform, jeans and a long-sleeved plaid flannel shirt. Although it looked like he was wiping down his truck in the drying bay, he was just staring at me with such intensity that I couldn't move, but I quickly turned my head to avoid his gaze. A split second later, in fear, I turned my head back to look at him. No one was there. The bay was empty, and I hadn't heard the noise the large car wash door makes when it goes up and someone leaves.

Almost a year later, in October of 2004, I had just returned from Paris and was getting myself ready for my daughter's wedding. I was slowly coming off my second round of prednisone and was increasingly optimistic that this time it would work, and I'd be healthy again. This gave me a new lease on life, but I fully realized that you can't move your life forward if you are firmly planted in the same place. I needed to hit the reset button, but I had no idea what that would look like.

The cabin I had planned to build and move into no longer excited me. In fact, I had decided to put the property up for sale. But where would I go? I could go absolutely anywhere. There was no reason I had to stay in Winnipeg or even in Manitoba. The world was at my feet. So, where did I decide to look first? Kenora, Ontario, a mere 120 miles and a two-hour drive from home. I wasn't aiming very far but at least I was looking in another province.

My friend Vlieta heard of a condo complex that was being built on Lake of the Woods and we decided to take a drive to Kenora, look at the property and the building plans, and have lunch before returning home. It would be a trip that would change us both.

We arrived at the real estate office and met with the agent, who asked us to follow him to the property. It was on the water's edge and would be a beautiful location for a condo if I was able to get one of the higher floors, to take advantage of the views. Vlieta had more than her share of spooky things in her life so she was fully aware of my burgundy truck experiences. We laughed when we pulled up to the property and the agent pulled in front of us driving a black F150. "Thank heavens his truck isn't burgundy," I said, "or I would feel forced to sign up and purchase a condo."

We got out of the of car and walked the property for a few minutes. There was nothing there yet. The units had just begun to sell, so the property hadn't been fully cleared. All we could see were small mounds of earth created by a small bulldozer which was left on the site. There were no other people around. The agent gave us some details. We had the brochures and information in our hands, so I just had to explore this a lot further. We said our goodbyes and got into my SUV. The agent was ahead of me so I looked in my rearview mirror so I could back up and then pull out. A burgundy F150 had just pulled up behind me.

There were two men inside and the man who was driving had a head full of silver hair.

We drove down a small hill and did a sharp U-turn and back up the hill, passing the spot where we had been parked. We were passing the burgundy truck very slowly. I could not look at the men but could sense they had gotten out of their truck and one had walked up the hill just ahead. We were going only about 10 mph, as it was a mud road and fairly narrow and steep. When we got to the top of the hill, Vlieta, who had not put on her seatbelt yet, was turned sideways and looking at me in horror.

She exclaimed, "Did you see him, did you see him?" She was panicked and started to really cry, so I stopped and put the car in park. "Did you see him? Did you see that man?"

All I could manage was to ask, "Was he wearing jeans and a long-sleeved plaid shirt?"

Yes, he was, and we watched the goose bumps and hair on her arms rise. We didn't look back. We couldn't look back. I was absolutely terrified and both of us were frozen in the moment. Vlieta, still crying, said, "Did you look at him, did you see his eyes? He was staring right at you, almost touching the side window, and his eyes were full of fire and light!"

We don't know what happened to us that day, who or what we saw or what it was supposed to mean. Was I to purchase the property and move, or wasn't I? I will probably never know. What I do know is some day, when I cross over to the other side, Dennis will be there to greet me and he'll say, "So what did you think of that magic trick I pulled on you in Kenora?"

## 40 – Walker

He thought he was invisible, but many eyes were upon him. His name wasn't Bob or Jim or Dave. I didn't know his name and I am sure his last name wasn't Walker. It's the name I gave him because that is what he did—he walked. The first time I saw him, shortly after moving to Hamilton Ave, was in 1997. He was walking down Ness, which ran east and west. I don't remember the day or the time of year, but Walker definitely caught my eye. It was the beginning of a relationship that would take me on a journey, walking with him. Not hand in hand or side by side but very much in his shoes.

I found out that Dennis noticed him too. We didn't make the connection right away but one day as we were driving down Ness, I noticed that we both turned our heads to watch him as we passed by him. Walker's life was a struggle. He had a desperate look of pain on his face and he walked with a debilitating limp. It seemed more like he was dragging his leg, and now I cannot even remember which leg it was. It was a visible struggle for him, day in and day out, every time I saw him. Who was this man? What was his story? Was he born with a limp? Did he always have difficulty walking or was this the result of an accident or surgery? I would never know and none of that mattered. The fact that he walked continuously and a long distance in every kind of weather told his story. Walking was a physical challenge. He was in pain and I am certain that emotional pain went with it, but for him walking was obviously therapy.

He was a big man, at least six feet tall, with a strong build and broad shoulders. His hair was thinning on top and you could tell even at a distance that he had not seen a barber in quite some time. His greying beard was gnarly and untrimmed. His clothing was sloppy and hung on him. None of that mattered to a man like him. He was on a mission. It was not to impress anyone, as he didn't know we were watching. He may not have been a man of means but he was rich in courage.

He simply walked. Up and down Ness, which runs past postwar homes at the beginning, then through Silver Heights and new builds from the '60s. So close to the airport runways and the Canadian Forces Base, you always felt you had to duck when planes were on a landing approach overhead. I would see Walker between Ferry Road and Sturgeon Creek, a good five-mile stretch.

Winnipeg is guaranteed extreme temperatures but that didn't stop Walker. Sometimes his beard would be covered with frost or frozen with snow. In pouring rain, summer heat or a prairie winter blizzard he walked. Weather conditions never stopped him. Over a great deal of time, he did improve but it was very slow. He never gave up even though this process took years.

I remember I was seeing him less because my life became too overwhelming to spend much time consciously looking for him. I did see him on that fateful day, June 30, 2000. I had been told that Dennis would die that day, so I remember the moment clearly. I was rushing home from the hospital to grab a bite to eat and let the dogs out. There was Walker. It brought a slight smile to my face to see him still around and having gained so much strength in his leg.

More time slipped by, and for me living had taken on a whole new challenge. Walker was still visible. Fortitude had replaced his limp and determination had never left his expression or demeanor. Six years had now passed since I first laid eyes on him. When for a few months I did not see him, my heart saddened. What if he was gone? What if something happened to him or he got so strong he gave up walking?

One day in August of 2004 I caught a glimpse of him as I was driving down Ness. He was on the opposite side of the street. I knew what I had to do the next time I saw him. I would be the one taking the big step. Later that fall I was all dressed up and on my way to a meeting and full of thoughts about the day. As I drove to my destination, I spotted him far ahead but walking towards me. Now was my chance and I could not let this opportunity pass. I made a quick right turn down a side street, another two right turns and I was back up at Ness, where he was walking across the intersection. I quickly parked the car and started to run down the street screaming at him,

"Stop, please stop," waving my arms to attract his attention. "I need to talk to you, stop please!" He stopped in surprise and turned his head to look at me. For a brief moment he probably wondered, "Who is this nut job in high heels chasing me?" I didn't care. I just had to catch up to him and when I did, severely out of breath, I just let it gush.

"I have been watching you for years and years and I know that I am not the only person who has seen your struggle and the remarkable improvement in your walking. What you don't know is that your journey has been an inspiration to me. While I was watching your progress, my own life fell apart. I battled a serious illness and recovered, only to be faced with a life-threatening kidney disease. I watched for you because you were the one person who could keep me going. I even saw you on the day my husband died in June of 2000. You showed me that by putting one foot in front of the other I could move my life forward no matter how great the pain. I needed to stop and take a moment of your time so that I could shake your hand and say that you have made a tremendous mark on my life and that I owe you a thank-you."

Walker was obviously stunned by my presence and what I had said. When I took his hand, his eyes welled up with tears. Then I said, "You will never know what you have meant to me and just how much you have done for me. From the bottom of my heart, I want to thank you." A tear trickled down his cheek as I turned and walked back to my car. He was a simple man who walked to heal himself. How fortunate I was to be able to tell him that he had helped me heal too. People come into our lives for a reason, a season or a lifetime and we find that our greatest lessons are found in the smallest of details.

I moved away the next spring and I never saw Walker again.

# 41 – Making my Move

Both of my children thought my moving to Kenora was a terrible idea. To their horror I put a $10,000 deposit on the property. I really didn't know what I was supposed to do. If Dennis was sending me directions, he certainly wasn't being very clear. Fortunately, I was able to get my deposit back after two months when I agreed that Kenora wasn't the place for me.

Every year we had the same Tarot card reader, and four years in a row she told me I should be living on Vancouver Island. I felt now was the time to check that out. My daughter had just been married and forty-eight hours later, in the middle of a snowstorm I flew to Victoria to see what the attraction was and why someone who really knew nothing about me kept telling me that I should be living there.

My friend Geoff Smith picked me up at the airport, and as I was walking very slowly and carefully out to his car he turned and asked me why I was walking so funny. I could see that the ground was wet, and I told him I didn't want to slip on the ice. He laughed and said, "We don't have ice here!" Victoria was lush and green and warm and beyond anything I could have dreamed, and to think that winter had already sat herself down on the prairies. I was immediately overwhelmed by the beauty of the architecture in this incredible city by the sea. I'd booked an ocean view room at the beautiful Laurel Point Inn and I was in paradise.

I had dinner with a long-time friend, Paulette, who invited me to housesit for her just before Christmas. This way I could see what Victoria was like midwinter. In December it was just as green and almost as warm as it had been in October. I went for long walks and shopped in the local stores, dined at fabulous local restaurants and fell more in love with the city. But I was a long way away from making any kind of permanent decision about a move further west, and I still didn't understand why I should be there.

Two months later, the company I worked for had their annual conference in Vancouver for only the second time in the company's history. Looking back, I see that as the turning point in my life and the path I was destined to take. If there was no conference in Vancouver that weekend, the life I'm now living never would have never happened. Before I went to Vancouver, I went to Victoria again for a closer look—this time with a list of ten homes and a real estate agent to help me. I thought perhaps when I was older, I could retire there.

I was staying with my friend Paulette, so she came along to help with the search. We went through the first seven homes pretty fast. Then we hit house number eight, and everything changed. It was a brand-new town house on a golf course and was set up as a show home. I was completely stunned. The style was West Coast Craftsman, which I'd never seen before. I can't explain how and what I felt, but both Paulette and May (my agent) knew I was in trouble. There was no point looking at houses nine and ten. I simply knew I was supposed to be there. It was overwhelming. I didn't sleep that night and phoned my financial planner first thing in the morning to see if I could do this. No problem. We went back to see the home again, but this time I saw the one next door and I fell even more in love.

I decided to take my life in a different direction by purchasing that house. For the next two hours a lot of running back and forth had to be done, as I had a ferry to catch to Vancouver at 4 p.m. The builders and their agent came to the show home for me to sign some paperwork and when it had been completed, I stepped out into the courtyard and will never, as long as I live, forget that moment. When Dennis was terminal he listened to Celtic and bagpipe music, which he loved, almost every day. When I stepped outside my new home the air was filled with bagpipe music. I don't mean from an open window or someone's car radio, it was everywhere, and it was loud.

We drove slowly out of the area and passed the Commonwealth Pool, which was built for the Commonwealth Games in 1994. In the parking lot there must have been sixty pipers in kilts and formation practicing for some event. In the eight years I lived there I never saw or heard them again. If that wasn't a sign that I was supposed to be there I don't know what was.

None of my friends could believe what I had done. I only knew two people on Vancouver Island, but that Tarot reader told me I was supposed to be there, and for some reason I too believed that's where I belonged. I had no idea if this was a good idea or a bad. I simply had to accept it for the adventure it was going to be.

I put my home up for sale and sold all my furniture. If I was starting fresh, I was also going to start with everything new. I had never lived anywhere else, so this was my new beginning. There were many farewells, but no tears were shed on my part. My Bichon Mozart had died the previous November and the very next day I found a six-week-old, two-pound baby girl Bichon. I named her Kismet, which means fate or destiny, and it was truly destiny that brought us together.

June 9, 2005 was my fifty-fifth birthday. My SUV was loaded to the top and my house was empty, as the movers had left the day before. I stayed with a neighbor but couldn't sleep. I had my whole future ahead of me. Shortly after sunrise Kizzie and I buckled up our seatbelts and headed west. I never looked back.

After a stop to see my daughter's university graduation, and a stop at my mom's in Kelowna so she could meet her new grand dog, our last day of the drive was to Vancouver, from where we took a two-hour ferry ride to the island. As we drove off the ferry and down the highway to our new home I was squealing with delight. A new life lay ahead. Who knew what it had to offer or where it would take me or why I was supposed to be there?

# 42 – Hotel Adele

My parents had owned our family business since 1960 and entertained clients long before I did. When clients came to town, even with their children, everyone stayed in our "rec room" downstairs. We also had a summer cottage where we spent weekends. Because I was the only child, my parents would have me bring a friend along. They also would invite their friends for the weekend; having a lot of people around was the norm for me. I've always felt that I was born with the hospitality gene. But one time I think I went a bit too far.

When I was in grade eleven, I was invited, with one of my girlfriends from school, to a party in another town. A boy band from North Dakota was playing two gigs in town and they just happened to be at the afterparty the same time as we were. Now this was 1967; and although it was the '60s, we were all really good kids. The boys in the band had short hair and wore beautiful suits, and I never saw or heard of any drug use whatsoever. From that time on, whenever they were playing in Winnipeg, I went to see them. Called "The Trade Winds 5" they had a great sound and played a mean Sam and Dave and The Four Tops. In the late '60s they launched a popular single that I heard on the radio.

One February my girlfriend Louise and I went to hear them play at a local high school. My parents were in Mexico on a holiday, and they had an elderly neighbor friend, Mrs. Fraser, stay at the house to keep me company and make sure I got to school on time. Since it was the weekend, I sent Mrs. Fraser home to be with her husband, and Louise was staying for a sleepover. It was Winnipeg in winter and typically it was around -40 °F. The band traveled in an old school bus which had no heat. We saw them on the Friday night, and they planned to drive a hundred miles overnight to play at an Armed Forces base. Teenage boys aren't too bright about health and safety, and I knew that if they encountered mechanical trouble with their old bus, they could all freeze to death by the side of the road. At their break and because they now knew me by name, I invited them to follow me home and stay at my place for the night. Okay, so fifty years later and even the very next morning I realized that wasn't such a good idea, but I was really more concerned about their welfare than my own. Like I said, I have the hospitality gene, which comes with a great deal of trust.

Where did they sleep? Two guys were in my mom and dad's double bed with our dog, one guy on the living room couch, I think, and three in the basement. To say that they were grateful is an understatement not only because of the weather, but because they were never in the same place long enough to have a business meeting. They asked Louise and me to excuse ourselves so they could talk, so we spent most of the time upstairs just staring at each other. My dad had a fully stocked bar downstairs, but no one touched a bottle. A couple of them may have been smokers but since there was no smoking in our house no one did.

The next morning Louise had to be at work by eight o'clock, so she left me with "the boys." They were clean-cut young gentlemen, and my only regret is that there was no food in the house—and even if there had been, I didn't know how to boil water. They must have been starving. Then there was a knock at the back door and my heart stopped. It was our neighbor Mrs. Leavens, whom I adored. She needed to get her car out of her garage and asked if the boys could move their school bus around to the front of the house. I thought I would die. Caught red-handed!

I still have the photos I took that morning, which remind me of a very innocent time in my life. The boys were so thrilled to have a place to stay for the night that they phoned a DJ at CKRC and had a song dedicated to me. It was "Sitting on the Dock of the Bay" by Otis Redding. I will never, ever forget it.

One week later my parents returned from their trip and while still in the airport arrival area I said, "Sit down, there is something I have to tell you." I was immediately grounded for three weeks, but later I too was rescued. Mrs. Leavens came over to talk to Mom and Dad and I expected even more punishment after she left, but to my great surprise my punishment was lifted. Mrs. Leavens, bless her, told Mom and Dad that they had raised me well and explained what happened.

She said those young men would have frozen to death if I had not taken them in. I was indeed a good Samaritan.

I raised two teenagers who were from time to time required and allowed to stay home alone. But I put the fear of God into them with the command, "No boys, no bands, no buses."

For thirty years Dennis and I entertained clients a lot, and at times I felt that I was running a boarding house. Some were regulars and some people I had never met. Offering our home was simply something we always did.

Some people never ever have house guests. But for me it is a very natural thing to do. I had so many house guests, both friends and relatives, visit me in Victoria that my neighbors renamed my home Hotel Adele. Call me crazy, but once I started my internet dating search, I opened my home and extended my hospitality to some men I met online. Not many, mind you, only a select few—the first being "Stinky Pete."

## 43 – A Cast of Characters

I threw myself into my new life in Victoria with enormous enthusiasm. Since I didn't know many people, I was determined to socialize and create a busy life. I joined Newcomers, which was the best thing ever. In that group I had my first golf lessons and joined the Monday golf group. I tried the gardening club, but my thumbs weren't green enough; took part in the single women's dinner club and movie night; and for Kismet we joined the dog walking group immediately so she could make friends too.

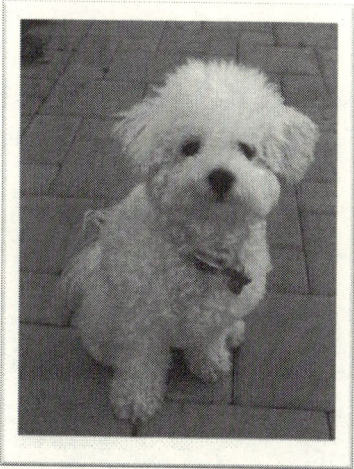

My sweet little Kizzie, now all of eight pounds, looked like a little bunny and was as fast, and that was a worry. One day she bolted, and I went on a terrifying search, afraid that she'd been picked up by an eagle. That was a common event in Victoria, and I lived near Beaver and Elk Lakes where they were often seen. Fortunately, that day a neighbor recognized her having a party on the fourth hole of the golf course. I realized I had to be proactive, so I enrolled us both in a puppy training class. That didn't sit well with Kizzie, and the first night she would not take part or even look at me. Instead, she sat on all the other dog parents' knees. At the end of the six-week course she was given a participation ribbon and we were invited back for another six-week session free with the hope that she would learn something. After our second six-week class Kizzie earned her second participation ribbon.

After my first year in Victoria, I began a seven-year journey with a volunteer job with Wear2Start, which proved one of the biggest blessings in my life. Having been in the fashion world, this was a perfect fit for me. Wear2Start helps women who have seen the harder side of life and now have been retrained for the workforce. They have resumes in hand, but they have nothing to wear for their interviews. Two to three days a week we gave these women the fabulous makeover experience with clothing donated by stores or Victoria citizens. We also had hairdressers who would donate their time to create a new look for our clients. I loved being a Tuesday girl and in 2007 I was able to receive on behalf of the organization a grant of $6000 from the eWomen Network in Dallas, TX. This gave us the opportunity to create a great boutique atmosphere for our clients where happiness happened every single day.

Now that I was living my new life, I fully realized how nice it would be to have a gentleman as a companion again, so I joined an internet dating site. It would be the first of many. I'll just call it "catch.com." I also joined a couples' dinner club where four men and four women would meet at a pre-selected restaurant with the hope of making a connection with someone. Women had to pay to join but men joined for free—a clear sign that the male population was slim. I found it was also a clue that they weren't too fussy about who they let in. I don't think you were supposed to cry all the way home after each dinner, but I did. I soon learned that some of these "gentlemen" had hotel rooms already booked and went for dinner with the goal of getting lucky. This was not for me.

My first two coffee dates from catch.com were epic. Date #1 was a widower and we met at a local marina. The only communication had been in writing. It was a really good thing we did meet, because my first fall and winter in Victoria was a real test of my endurance, and just thinking about this date later, during those rainy months, had me hysterical with laughter. He was a Japanese flamenco dancer wearing a French beret. I couldn't think of a single thing to say to him.

Date #2. OMG! It couldn't have gone worse; and all these years later I still crack up when I think of it. I'll just call date #2 Wolfgang. He was European and quite distinguished looking. Again, we never talked on the phone. It was only through catch.com messaging. He wanted to meet for coffee at Costco in Nanaimo. I had just moved to the island, didn't have a clue where Nanaimo was or how long it would take to get there, but I was up for an adventure. I would soon learn that Nanaimo was 70 miles north and an hour and a half hour drive from my home. After two hours of driving and a wrong turn I realized I had missed my destination. Wolfgang called me to say he'd finished up at Costco so could we meet for coffee at Home Depot. Hey big spender!

I soon saw a sign that said Courtenay/Comox, which was another hour north of Nanaimo and I knew I was really lost. I phoned Wolfie who told me to sit tight and he'd come out to the highway and find me. After twenty minutes he showed up and I followed him back to an actual coffee shop. Once we sat down the very first thing out of his mouth was, "So, vat are you doink for sex?"

Are you kidding me? I gulped my coffee down as quickly as I could and, after a very brief conversation, I told him I had to head home and I bolted.

We all know that karma is said to be a bitch, and I am pleased to say that Wolfgang got what was coming to him. Our date was in July of 2005 and because I will never forget him, I recognized him the minute he walked up the driveway to my garage sale in the summer of 2016. I didn't say anything. I was surprised to see him and kicked myself later for keeping quiet; but two years later in 2018, when he showed up to my garage sale again, I was not going to miss a second opportunity. I told him we had met before and he looked at me like I'd lost my mind and said he didn't think so. I reminded him of the coffee date in Nanaimo, and still in denial he said, "So vat kind of car was I driving?"

"A Jeep Grand Cherokee,"

"Vat color?."

I had no idea there was going to be a test, but I remembered and said, "Metallic gold or a light yellow." He was speechless, which gave me the upper hand, and I said, "You know, Wolfgang, in all my years of internet dating you have the distinction of being the rudest, most classless asshole I ever met!"

Wolfgang may have been the first jerk, but he wasn't the last. I was told that I was too old, too fat, that I had false teeth, wore a wig, and if I showed more cleavage, I'd get more action. There was also the man who put his hands on my waist and said, "I might want to fuck you if you lost thirty pounds." There was the guy who could only talk about my pretty toes and the color of my nail polish, and the one who looked like he'd been stung by 100 bees. One of my favorites was a self-described "entrepreneur" (that is why we met) who turned out to be a window washer with no employees. There was a very intelligent intellectual who didn't have a chin; and an accountant who took me out for dinner, insisted we order the cheapest item on the menu, and wanted a kiss at the end of the evening. I've also had notes from men who were very specific: "If you have any pets, don't bother writing," or "If you weigh over 120 lbs I don't want to hear from you." I had coffee dates during my travels too. Several when I visited my daughter and grandchildren, a couple in Vancouver, and a very funny one in Kelowna when I visited my mom. There had been a big snowstorm during the night and the man I was to meet for coffee kept delaying the meeting time because he had car trouble. When we finally did meet at a coffee shop, he went on and on about not being able to start his car and what a terrible day he'd had. I said, "Sorry, I win. My mother and I leave for Mexico tomorrow and this morning my dog ate her hearing aid."

Then there was the golf pro I met for a glass of wine. He was a very nice man, and we had a lot to talk about. How would I like a putting lesson? We met the next Sunday afternoon and I promised him that I would whip up some beans and weiners, which was a joke, for Sunday dinner afterwards. We met at the Ridge Golf Course putting green and he wanted me to putt to the farthest hole. I couldn't believe it, but the ball went in! He threw his arms in the air and said, "You don't need me." And my reply was, "I need a lottery ticket."

We went back to my place where he wrote down all the steps to a good putt. I'd gone out to the back yard and cut some twigs and branches to create an autumn centerpiece. The table was set with my best china, silver and crystal, making it appear as if it had been sprinkled with Martha Stewart dust. Because that's what I do. We had dinner, he didn't want wine, and before I could even serve dessert, he threw up his hands and said, "I can't do this! I've been divorced a couple of times, I'm just renting, and I have no money." With that he got up, grabbed his jacket and left. Never saw that guy again.

Standing out among this cast of characters was "Stinky Pete," the first man to get an invitation to my home. He was 6'2", divorced, and he golfed and lived on the BC mainland. He was ruggedly attractive and someone I began communicating with ten months after moving to Victoria. There wasn't an attraction on my part, but there was interest because after our first phone conversation we discovered that his best friend growing up was a business friend of Dennis's. This friend helped my son enormously after his dad died, and he had just died of cancer himself. That was too big of a coincidence to ignore, so Peter got the first invite to my home—for two nights in the guest room and a round or two of golf. I went to pick him up at the ferry and he walked right past me. That was because I was looking for someone 6'2" and he was closer to 5'9." He also came as a walk-on to the ferry because he was too cheap to bring his own car. I should have let him keep walking. Then when we stopped for lunch he said, "Do you mind if I have a cigarette?" He lit up that cigarette, after posting a profile that said "non-smoker." I should have taken him straight back to the ferry. But, silly me, I took him home.

He failed to bring a gift, not even a bottle of wine, and when he hung his jacket on the banister and used the washroom there was a horrible smell. I gingerly approached his jacket and had a whiff. OMG! It smelled like he'd been rolled in curry and slow roasted. Change of plans—the steaks went back in the freezer and out came the burgers. No silver, crystal or good china for this guy. Instead, I used the "I don't give a crap" décor.

I wasn't afraid of him. He was very nice, educated, and I had done my Google search, so I knew about his career. He hadn't lied about that. I made an excuse that I had to go next door to see my neighbor's new drapes. I needed help with what I should do next. We were going golfing in the morning, so I asked my neighbor to join us. Pete did turn out to be a terrific golfer, but his golf bag was filthy, disgustingly filthy.

My neighbor asked him, when I was out of range, how long he was staying, and his answer was, "Whenever she throws me out." I got it right away—he was a moocher. After the game I told him he'd be on the next ferry. In shock he asked what he'd done wrong.

My reply: "I don't think you can handle the truth, but a haircut and clean shoes go a long way with me."

Once he was gone, I sent him an email and really let him have it. He wrote back an apology saying that after spending his working life in a three-piece suit he realized he'd let things go and become far too casual. He actually thanked me for bringing it to his attention. That Christmas I got a card that said, "Thanks for the memories!"

## 44 – Catch and Release

I have always believed that people come into our life for a reason, a season or a lifetime, and that we are here to teach some and learn from others. As a woman in her mid-fifties who had never been on her own, I really had some lessons to learn and had to figure out who I really was. As a married woman for thirty years, friendships did not take priority; it was family always. Now it was relationships and friendships with both men and women that counted equally. I didn't realize it at first but exposing myself to internet dating was an excellent way to figure out who I was and what direction I wanted life to take. As we've all experienced, lessons can be painful, and this was the big one for me. I wasn't exactly free-spirited. I was more regimented and finding someone who could live up to my standards would be the enormous challenge.

Over time I began to see that some of the men I was connecting with really had a purpose in my life even if they weren't "keepers." The majority provided simple comic relief: but I learned a lot from them just the same.

I kept believing that there was someone out there for me, and that's how I met a lovely man named Dennis. I invited him to come from Vancouver for two days of golf. We had a very nice time and he offered to do any repairs I had around the house because, he said, single women had lots of them. He brought me a lovely gift and took me out for dinner. But there was no connection and there could never be. He was bald and had recently lost a lot of weight, so his clothes hung on him. All I could see was the resemblance between him and my late Dennis. The name being the same didn't help. He'd been widowed then married too soon afterwards, which ended in a divorce and cost him a great deal financially. I learned about timing and not to look for something that wasn't there.

Then Tim showed up. He was a golf pro who was going to be in town to visit family and wanted to meet up with a gal simply to try out some of the local courses. He may have been from "down East" but the very strange thing was, I knew his ex-wife who lived in Victoria. Before we met at the golf club, I invited him for dinner so we could have more time to talk. He told me he had been an alcoholic and had been thrown out of almost every dry-out facility in Ontario. He told me he finally stopped drinking when he learned how to feel. To really feel and deal with how and why he'd been so self-destructive, he had to open raw emotions that had never been dealt with. That really resonated with me because of Dennis's addiction and his pattern of self-destruction. It was only when both men finally faced their demons and opened up that they were healed.

Next was Bob. He lived "up island" and was a golfer who also liked to fly fish. We corresponded while I traveled to Maui to stay with a girlfriend and golf. We finally got to meet on my return.

The night before our date I had an unfortunate incident when the crown on my front tooth completely broke off when I bit into a frozen cookie. I called Bob and told him the date was still on, but I couldn't laugh at any of his jokes and I would be sipping soup. While having lunch we talked about my trip to Maui, when he suddenly said the name of the friend I'd stayed with. He knew her and her husband when they lived in Calgary and had even rented the condominium I had just stayed in. Again, the world keeps getting smaller. He was a very nice man and I kept hoping something would click between us, but it never did.

Then it got even stranger. Three weeks later Bob took off to mountain climb on one side of the world and I went off to Dubai and Egypt with a friend. On our second afternoon in Egypt, I was on a boat cruising down the Nile River when I saw a rock on the shore that was sprayed with blue paint and the words "Bob Maui." I was flabbergasted! Didn't have a clue what that meant but thought I needed to test this... was it a sign? On our next stop we spent most of the day in the ruins of the Karnak Temple. There was an ancient rock that could grant wishes and we were to walk around it many times, telling the gods our request. I decided to video our procession around and around the rock. My question, really with tongue in cheek, had to be: "Is Bob the man for me?" When I went to review the video immediately after it finished taping, it had disappeared. I took over 500 photos and videos during those three days and it was the only thing that got deleted. I guess I got my answer, because I never saw Bob again.

As if the pickings weren't slim enough, I met not one but two gentlemen whom I admit to seeing more than a few times, and both these men sent me into a tailspin. The first one, after a perfectly lovely evening, suddenly announced that he didn't know what the point to living was and that he was going to kill himself. We parted ways shortly thereafter. The second told me that although we were not going to continue seeing one another, he had made a new will and I would be named in it. He told me he wouldn't be living long and was planning his suicide. He was a jogger and planned to hire a truck driver who could run him down on a dark evening on an abandoned street. How on earth do you respond to that? As someone who has lost a loved one to suicide, you do not play around with that word anywhere near me. Both men broke my heart, but I learned with each one that I had actually dodged a bullet.

## 45 – End of an Era

The financial crisis of 2008 affected people near and dear to me. My childhood friend of over forty-five years lost her business, her building and her home. The fashion company I had been with for sixteen years had to close their doors when foreign banks called their loans. I certainly didn't think it would affect our family business.

In January of 2008 I met a widower from Calgary. I liked this man and I was extremely hopeful. Mr. T flew to Victoria to take me to dinner and six weeks later he came for another visit. I went to Calgary in that period and we saw each other four times. I was really excited that I could have a future with him. On the morning of Monday, February 25 I was just rousing from my sleep, lying on my left side facing the wall, when I felt someone's arms around me and a kiss on my neck just behind my ear. I tried to move but was paralyzed. I tried to speak but no sound came out. I knew it was Dennis; I could tell by his touch. But some instinctive sense told me not to try to look at him or I'd be gone too. I kept trying to call his name, but nothing came out, even though in my head I felt like I was screaming it. My eyes were wide open. Suddenly there was a flash of light on the wall in front of me. As fast as it came it was gone and my body relaxed. I knew it was Dennis. I just knew he was kissing me goodbye. I thought about it all day and felt that he was giving me his approval now that I had found Mr. T. Now he could leave in peace.

I couldn't have been more wrong.

One month later I was back for another visit. Mr. T had decided that having been a widower for only two years, it was too soon to be in a relationship. We decided to give it some time. Upon my arrival at my daughter's home, I was told to call my son immediately. I was not prepared for what came next.

Our bank had called the company's line of credit. This was our ninety-ninth year in business. The industry had changed dramatically, and the struggle was constant. The Canadian and American governments had dramatically changed the laws for importing and exporting fur and feathered species. The great Canadian outdoors wasn't attracting sportsmen to fish and hunt as much as in previous history. Companies weren't taking their executives on deluxe reward fishing trips to Canada's North as they were in the 1980s and '90s. It also became a generational thing, where now dads took their sons golfing and not fishing. Fishing lodges, which were often family-run, were closing in record numbers because tourist travel was declining. In Canada sport fishing had become "Catch and Release." If you caught a trophy fish, you couldn't keep it, you had to release it live. That meant you couldn't take your trophy meat home and there was no trophy to display on your wall.

Dennis started reproduction fish in the mid-'80s. It was a great alternative and a fabulous solution, manufactured by foam injection machines. Even I couldn't tell the difference between a replica fish and a real skin mount. Once you caught your trophy all you had to do was measure it and take a photo for the correct coloring, and our taxidermy artists made an exact replica. But there was one thing we didn't see coming with the new millennium, and it would change the course of our business forever. Even Dennis could not have predicted the demise of the industry in this way. That one small thing that changed our world was the digital camera. Why would you go to the expense of putting a trophy on your wall when you could have dozens of photos of your trip, and your catch, in the palm of your hand?

My son and I made the decision to close the doors.

To say that this was the most difficult year of my life would be an enormous understatement. I now know that hug and kiss I felt from Dennis back in February was really an "I'm so sorry, Adele. You have no idea what's ahead." The first thing I had to do was sell the building, which I owned, so the bank could be paid back. My fear of not being able to sell it overwhelmed me. I imagined the cost of heat, insurance and taxes over a Winnipeg winter and I was afraid it could bankrupt me. Fortunately, the building sold by the end of July to the second person who looked at it; and upon inspection it had no asbestos in the ceiling or walls, or anything else that could jeopardize the sale. The new owners were wonderful and gave us until mid-December to empty the building.

We had absolutely no help from our lawyer, our accountant or our bank—a bank that we had been with longer than I had been alive. Not a phone call or a visit, and whenever I made a trip to the bank, the manager never showed his face. There was no empathy from that institutional pillar. When it was all said and done, I took a vow to close all my personal accounts there and never step foot in any of their branches. I was done! But, that bank bit me one more time. Several years later I applied for a credit card at an American department store and I was declined. I thought it was perhaps because I was Canadian. Several more years passed, and I applied for a credit card in a Canadian department store and I was declined again. What was going on? The store assured me I would get a letter from their credit department telling me why I was declined. Thank God I was sitting down when I opened the credit letter after it arrived. Apparently, I was dead.

It took months to figure out what had happened. In July 2000 when I went to the branch of the bank in question to tell them Dennis had died and to remove him from our bank accounts, they apparently ticked the wrong box, which killed me off instantly. Computers had changed a tremendous amount in fourteen years, but fortunately the branch manager remembered our family, so at least I didn't have to prove who I was. It took an entire year to straighten that mess out.

There was something else going on. I had booked a weekend in Dallas at the eWoman Conference, where I'd received the $6000 grant for my volunteer job. This would be the third time I attended, but this time I had no interest in whatever was going on. I just needed a rest and a break from all the chaos in my life. I hoped a few days of sleep in the comfort of a luxury hotel would give me the strength to return home and face the future. I flew to the conference with some girlfriends, but I was too exhausted to attend the first two evenings.

On the Saturday morning, at the last minute and because I was already awake, I went to hear the morning speakers. I only remember

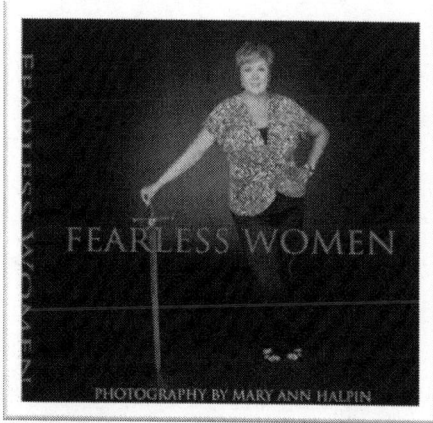

one, Mary Ann Halpin. She is a photographer who told her story and was putting together photo books of Fearless Women, many of them famous. For a fee she would do your portrait with the same sword that all the women in the book had held. Some of the fee would be going back to the organization for their grant program. I had to do this. It was like something overpowered me, and when the session ended, I ran to where I could sign up. To get through the next six months I needed to be strong and fearless. I was very determined. I stood in line for two hours and was the second to last person signed up.

The next morning my friend Val and I met with Mary Ann and her husband Joe. I was so rattled that I didn't have a clue how I should stand or what to do with the sword. Time was a factor, so it went by in a blur and I was a wreck. In the end it was Joe and my friend Val who insisted on the picture chosen. Because I bought the large portrait, I would also receive the book with my picture on the cover. In this particular photo I looked relaxed and at peace, as if a job had been well done and I was simply leaning on my sword as if I had just conquered the world. This book is truly what saved my life over the next six months. I was now a fearless woman. I looked confident and in control in the photo, and every single morning I would look at the picture and into my own eyes and say, "How do you eat an elephant? One bite at a time." I would get through this!

The first level of pressure was lifted when the building sold, but now the real work had to begin. We had a three-story building and warehouse. Over 16,000 sq ft. There were records going back to the '70s, which all had to be shredded. I have never worked so physically hard in my entire life and I was fifty-eight years old. All of our staff had left us, and we couldn't afford to hire people to help us clear the building because they would not have been covered by workman's compensation if they were injured. There was just my son and I, plus one girl in the office and one man in the back to help us. You really find out who your friends are when you are in a time of crisis. Many came to help us haul out garbage and dismantle the place whenever they could. Even the friends who couldn't physically help kept me busy or entertained on weekends to give me a change of scenery. I am so grateful to those who helped, as I couldn't have survived without them. Kismet and I moved in with my brother-in-law for close to six months while we got the job done.

In mid-November my friends Penni and Gord came to help us for a day. We were in the back warehouse trying to move some machinery around. There was a huge frame made of cast iron that was about twelve feet long. We needed to move it out the shipping doors, as it was being sold for scrap metal. All we had to help us was a broken dolly, so the four of us moved it very slowly, because it weighed a ton. When we got to the doors, we were stopped by huge snowbanks outside and couldn't move any further. Together everyone lowered the frame, right on to my left foot. Penni said afterward that she had never heard a scream like that in her life. I was sure all of my toes had been amputated and I was screaming in pain. I was helped to a barrel so I could sit down, but before I could get there a powerful wave of heat like a blast from an industrial furnace hit me full force, throwing me backwards slightly. Once seated I just stared at my left running shoe waiting for blood to gush out. Nothing happened, so I unlaced the shoe and removed my white sock. There wasn't a single mark on my foot. I wiggled my toes, no pain, I stood up, no pain; I walked a few steps, no pain. I went right back to work and stood for over eight hours that day and I even went swimming later that evening. I never lost a toenail and didn't even have a bruise. One more spooky thing had just happened.

By the beginning of December, we were organized enough to have an auction. We had a building full of things we needed to get rid of, and the money earned would go right to the bank. I had two very personal items that I needed to part with and asked the auctioneer if they could be listed for sale as well. The auctioneer felt sorry for me and said he wouldn't charge me a commission on my personal items. One was the brass bed that Dennis had paid $2000 for back in 1979.

After he passed away, I couldn't look at it again and had been storing it in our mezzanine for eight years. Neither of my children wanted it, as it reminded them too much of their dad being sick. The other item was an incredible roll-top desk that was over a hundred years old, which Dennis had purchased also for around $2000. We used it for many years, but it couldn't be wired for computers, so instead it held a place of honor in our boardroom. It was beautiful but too big to move anywhere.

We held the auction on Saturday, December 6 and the place was packed. We raised far more money than the auctioneer had anticipated. The two items I had for sale went as well. Sadly, the bed sold for only $80 but the antique desk went for $1300. The same gentleman bought both and offered an apology to my son for paying so little for two such valuable items. Later Damien came to me and said that his dad would roll over in his grave if he knew what they sold for.

On the Monday morning the auctioneer arrived with two cheques. One for the business inventory and a personal cheque for me. I was absolutely stunned when I saw the amount in writing. My total was $1380. This number was significant to me because from 1974 to 2008 the business was located at street number 1380. There was no question in my mind that Dennis knew what we were doing.

Our family business was his life. Everything else came second to the company. It provided employment for hundreds over the years and an excellent income for my parents, who could afford to retire at the age of fifty-five. The company gave Dennis and me and our children a life free of financial worry. But because the business came before us, we all suffered. On Monday, December 15, 2008 everything was gone. Damien and I walked out the front door and I locked the building for the very last time. Two weeks before our one hundredth year. It's been twelve years now and I have not had one single moment of Dennis spooky shit since then. Not one. He is truly gone. Locking the doors and walking away for that last time ended an era and his soul was finally set free.

## 46 – A Teenage Crush, Crushed

I knew Bill Badman growing up. I've changed his name to protect the innocent, but this man isn't innocent, and he rates a chapter all to himself. Bill lived on the next street and we had gone to the same elementary, junior high and high schools. As kids and preteens, he was part of our street crowd. We played hide-and-seek, Mother May I, or just hung out at the playground across from my house, "The Tot Lot." It was the '60s and streets were safe long after dark. Bill was just one of the boys, one year older and a grade ahead of me. Bill played in a band with some of the other guys from his school. On Saturday nights all the single girls went to the Perth Community Club to have fun, dance and try to meet boys. Bill's band often played there.

By the time we reached eighteen or nineteen we were out of high school, either in university or working. I was working in a department store and often saw Bill riding the escalator on Saturdays. We hung out together on weekends and went to Grand Beach almost every Sunday. Brian and Glenna were going steady, as were Debby and Gary. This was back when all the girls wore bikinis because we were skinny. We coated our bodies in baby oil and baked in the hot summer sun. Having never heard of skin cancer, we would flip over and bake the other side when the baby oil started sizzling. I was known for my perpetual tan, as I tanned easily. Bill and I were on our own and not dating anyone, but oh how I wished it was different. I had developed a huge crush on the guy. He was smart, terribly funny, tall, dark, and handsome, but he couldn't even look me in the eye. He was very shy and simply looked at his feet and kicked the ground whenever I was near.

On September 4,1971 Brian and Glenna were married and Bill was the best man and I was the maid of honor, so we got to walk down the aisle together. Eight weeks later I married Dennis and I never saw Bill again.

Fast forward to 2009. What could have possibly changed in almost forty years? For starters, I was widowed, and I had been living on Canada's West Coast since 2005. Before I left Winnipeg, I went to our high school reunion in 2003 and saw Gary, Brian and Glenna. Bill wasn't there. Brian and Glenna had been long since divorced; and in two years Glenna, who was one of my bridesmaids, would die suddenly from a heart attack. Both Gary and Brian had long and successful careers and had moved to other cities.

By 2009 I was all too familiar with the internet and found a site that helped you find old high school friends. I joined and looked through the unfamiliar faces. I did see Bill's name listed so I wrote him. Honestly, he was the only one I really was interested in finding. He wrote back right away.

It was now April 2009 and my daughter's twins were due shortly, so I was packing and heading to visit and stay a month or so to help her out. Bill lived in a city near her, so we exchanged numbers with a promise that since he was often in town, he would call and take me to dinner. Apparently, he had been divorced for many years.

I was back home in late June and never heard from Bill. In July I got a call with an apology from him for not calling earlier. He told me he had a very visible and important government job and was incredibly busy. We chatted a long time, catching up, then he asked if I was going to be home on the weekend. He said that he was going to send me something and "sweep me off my feet" and left it at that. All weekend I watched for a delivery and put a note on the door when I was out of the house. Nothing arrived. So much for sweeping. He had dropped his broom. Silence once again. I did not hear from Bill again until mid-December of 2009.

His reason for no communication was valid. I would learn much later that in late August he was struck down with H1N1 virus, which was shaking up the Western world that fall. He was in the hospital for an extended period of time and wasn't sure that he would make it out. An immediate retirement came next as his illness took its toll. Still at the email stage, he told me he had a time-share at the La Quinta Resort in Southern California—at least, that is what I heard him say. He knew I loved to golf and offered to be my host down there for a week in January. Friendship came first but we would see if we had a romantic connection.

My heart skipped a beat. This sounded perfect. I immediately Googled the La Quinta Resort and I was in. The resort was gorgeous. It was classy and beautiful, and I could think of nothing but romantic dinners and moonlight. He promised golf, shopping and sightseeing, adding that Palm Springs had a wonderful tram ride up the mountain.

Bill sent me flowers once I let him know I would join him in La Quinta. I learned that back in July, when he stated that he would be sweeping me off my feet, he had sent me a bouquet of flowers at that time as well. However, he didn't know my address, and had it delivered to someone else with the same last name, who kept my flowers.

I looked forward to his many phone calls and emails. We swapped pictures, and although his was just a head shot, he looked older but somewhat the same. I told everyone I knew about this matchup. I was truly over the moon. Bill was so thoughtful that he booked my flight to Palm Springs via another western city the night before we were to meet so that I could spend the night with my grandchildren.

He made me laugh. Those four weeks of waiting to leave flew by. I know I was a bit obnoxious on New Year's Eve when my friend Wendy and I went to dinner because I could talk of nothing else. I couldn't wait to get home and call him. Did I see any red flags? Not really... but perhaps there were two that I would call hot pink. Bill seemed a wee bit needy, with more than a few calls in a day, and if I didn't return his calls or answer his emails immediately, he questioned me about something being wrong.

I was also concerned about Bill's health and expressed my concerns to him. The virus that put him in the hospital in the fall sounded more severe than I had first thought. Apparently, the violent coughing spells he encountered caused a broken bone in his back. Slowly the truth came out. After many years of trying to figure out what was wrong with him, he was diagnosed with osteoporosis. I never knew that was possible for a man. According to him he was now a poster person for the disease and the University Hospital kept a constant check on him. He had broken many, many bones over the years from this disease, so he told me that he was an inch or two shorter than he used to be, but he assured me over and over that he was the picture of health.

Talking every night on the phone is a great way to get to know a person. With no outside interruptions I felt free to ask all sorts of questions, so we talked for hours every day. As time progressed the real truth came out, and it floored me. In 1969 when I had seen Bill so many times in the department store where I worked, it was because he rode the escalator on Saturdays to watch for me. Yes, he confessed that for most of our teen years he had a huge crush on me. He could even describe outfits that I wore forty years earlier. I admit that was a bit creepy. Apparently, everyone else knew, because when I wrote our mutual friend Gary to tell him we were meeting up, he wrote back to say how wonderful it was for Bill at this age and stage in life to be off vacationing with the girl of his dreams. Wow! To hear that confirmation felt amazing.

January 7 finally arrived. I had carefully chosen my travel wardrobe and packed and repacked obsessively. I took far too much luggage but brought candles, good placemats and dinner napkins. If we were eating in, I knew a time-share condo wouldn't offer much in the way of décor, so I added what I could. Bill had bragged that he was a gourmet cook and he really sounded as though he knew what he was doing in the kitchen.

I was so excited that I don't even remember my flight. My daughter picked me up at the airport and we had a lovely evening. The next morning, she dropped me back at the terminal and wished me luck. She was excited about my big trip too. I told everyone including the US customs gal who was patting me down. She asked if this reunion was going to be on Oprah. This was what I had been waiting years for, a partner in life. Who better than someone I had history with? Even if it had been forty years, people basically don't change, do they? Everyone sitting around me on my flight knew my story, and I asked the woman sitting next to me if she would take a picture of Bill and me when we met. Of course, she would. When the captain made the announcement to prepare for landing, I thought I would explode with excitement. This was it. All these years later I still can recall my descent from the boarding lounge to the lower level of the Palm Springs airport. Fortunately, it's not a large airport. We were to meet at the luggage area.

Five minutes later all I wanted to do was crawl in a hole and die. Oh fuck—Bill was short. I mean, 5 feet 3 inches. He told me he'd lost a few inches, but I remember him being close to six feet tall. I'm 5'5" and I had to bend my knees to be shorter than him when we had our photo taken. His leather jacket was probably the right size for his upper body, but because he was so short it hung almost to his knees. He had assured me that he was healthy, but he could hardly walk. He had obviously lied to me. In total shock, all I wanted to do was run—run far and run fast. I excused myself and ran off to the first ladies' room I could find. I phoned my daughter to tell her "This is NOT going to work!" But I had to go back. What was I going to do? We'd been together five minutes and it was obvious that he'd lied to me about his height and his health. I couldn't believe it, and my disappointment overwhelmed me. I simply didn't want to be there.

I had to do some serious positive attitude pep talking to myself. I had committed to an entire week with Bill, and although I instantly knew there would be no attraction, no romantic connection, I could still be a friend. But that was pushing it. I had been deceived and I just wanted to go home.

Bill said we were going to a fantastic resort: there would be sunshine, good food, and as promised, great golf in the days to come.

I thought: Put one foot in front of the other and smile. Just smile and act as if it's all good. No, it's great. It's all going to be great. A holiday in a beautiful resort with an old friend. What could go wrong?

It took what seemed like forever for the rental car to arrive. With no specific directions, just an address, we took off. It was getting dark and the drive was longer than I expected. It was darker than I was used to because there are very few streetlights in the desert. Around 5:30 p.m. we picked up the keys to our condo at an office in a local strip mall. Why would we do that if we were staying at the famous La Quinta Resort? That's when I learned there is a giant difference in the prepositions *the* and *a*. We were NOT staying at *The* La Quinta Resort, we were staying at *a* La Quinta resort. Turns out we weren't even in La Quinta. We were staying in Indian Wells. We arrived at our "resort" in the pitch dark and had to carry our own bags to the door—again, a clue that this wasn't a resort. Where was the doorman? This was a simple condo that had not been updated since it was built, which was probably in the '70s. Next shock, it was a dump, and I mean *dump*. I claimed the only bedroom. Bill had originally booked a studio suite, but I thought he was being a bit premature and had him change it to a one-bedroom. I didn't know where he was going to sleep. I didn't care. He would not be sleeping anywhere near me.

This was not the luxury resort he had promised. There was a very small fridge and kitchen sink, no counter space and a stove that wasn't much more that a hot plate. A table with four chairs, a couch, armchair and TV completed the living area. The bathroom had rusty taps and an old bathtub. The bedroom I took had no closet and a TV that didn't work. I would have to sleep diagonally because the springs were popping through the mattress. I felt that I had just arrived in a Third World country; but it never occurred to me to leave, to just call a cab and find a hotel of my own. I knew I would be breaking Bill's heart and really it was only for seven days; I could put up with anything for seven days. So, I made up my mind to stay. I now know I was in shock and denial, and I should have hightailed it out of there as fast as I could.

We needed food, so we got back in the car and found a grocery store within a few miles. Bill bought some wine and vodka, and a few food items including a roasted chicken and lettuce. There wasn't much chatter on the way home.

I slept terribly that first night. Bill was on the couch, which shared a wall with my bed. All night I could hear him hitting the wall or yelping out in pain. He sounded like a wounded animal. I was terrified. If my bed was old and uncomfortable. I could only imagine how broken down the couch would be. Bill had brought a small laptop and a bunch of movies we could watch. I bowed out and he watched them all night for seven nights. When daylight came, I could see that the entire community was gated, and we were surrounded by million-dollar homes and lush green golf courses. Bill had promised me golf, right? So, we would probably be golfing right around the corner. The Santa Rosa mountains rose up right in front of us. I'd never seen such beauty, and I had that stunning view to look at every day.

I didn't have cell phone service in the US, but I needed to make a few calls. First to the airline to change my return flight. Bill had been anticipating that our reunion would be one of romance, so he'd shared with me his plans for our return home. We would fly together to his city where we would be met by a limousine and taken to one of the luxury hotels where he'd booked the penthouse suite for our last night together. Well, you could bet big bucks that would NOT be happening. I phoned the airline and changed my return flight. I would go directly home.

My second call was to friend Debby from our teen years, who had encouraged me to make this trip with Bill. Having seen him career-wise over the years, she reminded me how smart and funny he was and that we would have a fabulous time together. That was obviously a very long time ago. She was now a psychologist, and I knew I would need her help, so I phoned and invited her to come for coffee the morning after my return. I knew I didn't just need someone to talk to, I would need a shoulder to cry on.

Bill heard me on the phone with the airline and things took another turn for the worse. When he realized that I really had no interest in him, this self-professed gourmet cook began to punish me with food. I kept waiting for this man to suggest dinner or lunch out, or perhaps golf or sightseeing. I was willing to pay my own way, but nothing, not a word. My disappointment was overwhelming.

Every morning I went to the pool in front of our suite and sat and stared at the mountains and the palm trees, and I stayed there for the entire day. The pool was small, but the weather was perfect, and I exercised in it every day. Bill came swimming a few times but hurt himself by jumping in the pool. He consumed a lot of vodka. One day he came home from grocery shopping and dropped a bag on the patio, leaving a new bottle of vodka shattered on the cement. I couldn't believe that he made no effort to clean it up. The job was left to me.

I only had a glass of wine each evening, as I had to keep my wits about me. I wasn't in any danger because in the past Bill had multiple bone breaks and I knew that if I felt threatened in any way, I could kick him in the shins and break a bone with my bare foot.

He went grocery shopping alone each morning. I wasn't allowed to go with him even though he could barely walk and was in a great deal of pain. On the Monday we went to a golf shop nearby, but he could only stand in the store five minutes before going back to the car to sit. I'd watched him dump morphine pills into the palm of his hand, then wash them down with straight vodka. He ran out of morphine by Tuesday.

On the Sunday, forty-eight hours after arriving, I had called some old high school friends who lived there in the winter. I really wanted to get together with them. Bill said he remembered them, but when I suggested dinner with them, he actually yelled at me, "Who's buying dinner?" I said that since they were all my friends, I would love to take everyone out for dinner. That's when he really screamed at me, "There's no goddamn way a woman is buying me dinner!!!" I froze. It was clear he didn't want anyone from the past seeing the way he looked now.

I went alone and met my friends on the Tuesday night. I failed to say anything to my friends over dinner. I simply gave the excuse that Bill wasn't feeling well. Why I didn't have my bags packed and with me so I could stay with my friends, I will never understand. I really think I was still in shock.

During the day Bill was on his cell phone constantly, so I asked if he had an American cell phone plan. He looked at me like I was nuts—

why would he need that? I explained that he would have an outrageous phone bill when he got home because he was phoning from another country. He was far from rich and I knew that this could be an issue. He ignored me and kept phoning. He said there was a problem at his old workplace, and he needed to check in on his former staff. When I returned from my solo dinner that evening, he was still on his phone and went outside to talk so I couldn't hear him. Those walls weren't too thick, however, and as he chatted outside my window, I could clearly hear what he was saying. I was frozen by what I heard. He was talking to another woman and using the exact same lines he had used on me. It appeared that he had met her at the grocery store. So that was why he went grocery shopping every day and wouldn't let me go with him, and why he came home with a fresh baguette every day. I finally got it. This man had said he wanted to renew a friendship, but he just wanted to get laid, and now he knew it wouldn't be with me.

Thursday, our last full day, I finally came clean about knowing there was another woman and suggested that he could take her out that night. I wouldn't mind. I actually said, "We haven't been anywhere. No golf, no dinner out, no sightseeing. Take your new girlfriend out for the evening."

He went into a rage because he'd been caught: "I've spent too much goddamn money on you!" That was his excuse, but I really didn't care. I went into my bedroom, closed the door and wept quietly while I packed my suitcase and counted the hours till my departure. I mentioned that this gourmet cook punished me with food. Well, the last day I got a hot dog for lunch and Kraft dinner for supper.

Friday morning, I was up early and ready to go. I'd told Bill my flight left three hours earlier than it actually did just so I could get out of there. Bill had changed his departure date because (he said) he wanted to go to the Bob Hope Golf Classic. I knew he would never be able to handle being a spectator at a golf tournament because you have to walk miles. Then I overheard that he was picking up the new woman after I left. I could've cared less. I drove us in the rental car to the airport. He had run out of morphine and was nasty, and I couldn't trust his driving.

At the curbside check-in, when I got my bags out of the trunk, I took Bill aside and told him that I had put the rest of my US cash, $400, in his coat pocket to help cover some of his expenses. He went ballistic. In front of everyone checking in he started screaming that I was a fucking useless drama queen.

When I finally arrived in my safe, warm home I spiraled downward. Even before I brought my luggage into the house I went in and erased all Bill's phone messages and emails. I tore up his picture and smashed the flower vase in the garbage. I told no one the truth. Instead, I sent out a general email stating that I had a wonderful time reconnecting with an old friend but had no love connection. It was months before I could even tell my daughter what had really happened. I was devastated and ashamed. I was smarter than that! I had asked the right questions, and as always, I did my Google research. How could I have been so blind and believed all the things he told me? Perhaps it was because I was lied to from the beginning.

I strongly believe that nothing in life is a coincidence. That week in La Quinta had happened for a reason. I now know that my time spent with Mr. Badman was actually a glimpse into my future. My future would be in La Quinta and my new life would be only a stone's throw away from where this all happened. The clock was ticking.

## 47 – It Sucks to be an Optimist

I was just about at the end of my rope in November of 2011 when a gentleman I'll call Tom contacted me on catch.com. At first, I couldn't find his profile because it had been sent to me previously, but I hadn't been impressed and I had deleted it. I reactivated his profile, we messaged a few times, and he asked if he could call me. He had a question for me and a first-class ticket on Alaska Airlines. Would I like to go to Cabo San Lucas, where he had a time-share, to golf for a week? I'd heard that line before. Remember going to La Quinta with Bill Badman to golf and sightsee for a week? We all know how that turned out. Do you really think I'd fall for that story again? Well, I did, and I said yes.

There was one giant condition that went with my agreement. I would pay for my own golf and my half of the meals and accommodations. And, I would have the master bedroom to myself. I know, I know… I still really shouldn't have done this. It's like that saying, "Been there, done that, should have known better the first time."

What I did get now were the names of the friends who would be joining us. There were three other couples, his very long-time friends. Tom had been a widower for almost ten years and his friends were along to support him. Believe me, I Googled him and his friends and found tons of information, so there was no question that he was who he said he was, and he was a very successful man.

I flew to another city to meet up with him, paying my own way there. My heart honestly sank when I saw how he was dressed. I had worked for an airline for many years in the '80s and we were required to dress appropriately for travel even if on another airline. To me travel is a privilege, so I still look my best when I'm on an airplane. This man looked like he had just taken out the garbage.

Unlike my last adventure, the resort we were staying at was fabulous. Our suite was huge, and I got the master bedroom, which was perfect. Up to that point I thought this was really going to be fun. We ate in the resort the first night and golfed the next day with one of the couples. I was very intimidated by the course, but I was fine, and his friends were delightful. I would be meeting the rest of the group that evening at a seafood restaurant and I was looking forward to it... but then, of course, something went very wrong.

It was Sunday afternoon, and as I was getting ready for our evening out, I could hear his phone pinging almost constantly. I asked what was going on and Tom said he was getting updated on the football scores. Once I was ready, I came out and sat at the dining room table to check my emails and he got up, put his phone on the table beside me and went to shower. His phone pinged again and because it was right beside me, I picked it up to take a look at who was playing and what the scores were, because I am a big football fan. It was not football scores but rather an instant message from a woman somewhere in the USA sending him her phone number so they could talk. We had only been there twenty-four hours and he was already casting his net further afield. I was ticked off. What was the point of me even being there? I asked Tom for an explanation but there wasn't one, nor was there an apology.

The weather could have been better that week, but I still spent most of my time around the pool alone. On the Tuesday night we went to a happy hour on the beach where Tom completely ignored me and left me by myself. I met a woman from Denver who'd had quite a bit to drink, and she was going overboard on how wonderful I looked. When Tom came by, she was gushing all over him, congratulating him on such a beautiful wife and how stylish I was. He never said a word, wouldn't even look at her. It would take seven days for him to say, "You look nice."

We played golf almost every day, and that was a godsend. On the Thursday he went golfing with the guys and I was to meet up with him in the bar when they were done. I got all dressed up and took a cab there but had to wait a long time before he showed up. We sat in the bar and ordered drinks, and he started up a conversation with two men a few tables away. It was all about football. Suddenly he got to his feet with drink in hand and went to sit with them to carry on the conversation. It was as if I didn't even exist. Each day he became ruder and I became more disgusted. We flew home on Saturday, December 10, and for the entire flight he read his book and never spoke to me once. At one point between 7 and 8 p.m. the pilot announced that on the right side of the aircraft you could see the lights of La Quinta, CA. I looked out the window and thought, I'll never, ever go back there, and now another vacation has been a total bust. Just before landing in Seattle I asked Tom if he would like me to have the pilot circle for an extra hour so he could finish his book. I was done.

I had been on catch.com for nine years. I couldn't find one nice guy to golf with. What I did find was a lot of fake people with made-up profiles. They could have been fifteen-year-old boys or men in prison or just plain nuts. I have no idea, but I reported hundreds and hundreds of fake men. I would start with Alabama and finish with Wyoming, searching each state and Canadian province. I was a detective for nine years. At the beginning of each page of profiles they would post the newest ones, and I soon caught on to the fact that the same pictures appeared in more than one state or province at the same time. If you read the introductions, there weren't just spelling mistakes but whole paragraphs out of context that didn't make any sense; and I began to realize that these were copied and pasted from someone else's profile. In many, the photos were too perfect. There would be a very good-looking man posing against a doorway with a cup of coffee in his hand and a big toothy smile. I didn't know if he was advertising coffee or toothpaste. They had been cut and pasted from magazines, and from the style and layout I could tell that they were most likely European magazines.

The one that really upset me, I still have. It was a fake profile of a widower who was fifty years old from Concord, NH. He said he had no children but posted pictures of him and a young boy. He said he was a non-smoking Christian, health researcher, 6'0" and looking for love. His profile name was "billionsmiles." This wasn't the first time I'd seen his photo and I'd reported him to catch.com many times. I cannot insert the picture here because the profile photo in question was of a former prime minister of Canada.

It really does suck to be an optimist, because when I joined these sites, I didn't pay for a year's membership to get a price break. I paid by the month, which was at times twice as expensive. Instead of getting a deal, I convinced myself that "next month" someone suitable would show up. I now had over $4000 invested in this scavenger hunt, and I kept coming up empty handed.

I tried other ways to meet members of the opposite sex. I joined three performance choirs that were mixed company. I took art classes and writing classes. I even took a class in pole dancing—I thought I could add a little spice to my life with a new "skill." I wasn't surprised when the other two girls in the class were in their early twenties, but I was surprised that I sprained my back in the second class and spent the next four weeks flat on my back on the couch, healing. In the end I decided to knock something off my bucket list, and I took up fly fishing. I thought that would be a fun way to mix with new people and hopefully men my age. Well, there was just me and eight old geezers. Our instructor, who was from Scotland, couldn't believe I was still single after twelve years and promised to find me a partner. He claimed that he knew fly fishermen all over the world. I kept practicing my technique on dry land and my rod and reel never even saw water.

I continued to put my "Top 10" list out to the universe and often would catch myself at a red light looking up at the heavens and rattling it off. But I always ended up saying, "Is anyone up there even listening?"

I was doing a lot of soul searching and trying to accept the fact that I would be alone for the rest of my life. I needed to give up this search, as there were no princes out there. One day, however, when I was visiting my grandchildren, three-year-old Ella said to her little sister, Kate, "Let's just lie here and wait for the prince to come and kiss us."

If only life were that simple.

## 48 – You've Got One Chance to Make a First Impression

January 2012 arrived and so did a bout of pneumonia. I was sick and miserable. I was still on catch.com and the two men I was corresponding with didn't give me a glimmer of hope. One sent me an inappropriate photo and the other lived somewhere in Oregon that I couldn't find on a map. I told myself: Give it up, Adele. Time to pull the plug on your catch.com search. But I made one change, to my profile photo. It was taken on my sixty-first birthday when seven of my girlfriends took me out for a fun evening of chocolate and champagne and being pampered with makeovers. Not bad, I thought, for a sixty-one-year-old.

My friend Carol had been in Vancouver for a week and decided to come to Victoria to check up on me. I was really too sick to do much, so we just sat and chatted for three days. On Saturday, January 28 at approximately 9 p.m. Carol sent me a text just after arriving back in Toronto. She told me an old high school friend named Barb Irving had been the flight attendant on the plane and asked me if I remembered her. I sent her a text back saying yes, I remembered her but hadn't seen her in over forty-five years. That text distracted me and instead of deleting my catch.com profile, which I had sworn all day I would do, I turned off my computer and went to bed.

As I was slowly waking the next morning, I startled myself when I realized that I had gone to bed without deleting my dating profile. I ran to my office, turned on my computer and started cursing. My account had automatically been renewed at midnight and another

$49.99 was charged to my credit card. I was so mad at myself that I stomped around all morning not believing I had been so stupid. Around 4 p.m. I made the decision to just accept the fact that I'd blown another $50 and remove my profile anyway. I simply had to get off the internet. This was a nasty, addictive process that led nowhere.

These dating websites post notifications when you have a message or even if someone has looked at your profile. I had been on catch.com for nine years and over 6450 men had looked at or read my profile. I sat down to pull the plug, and sure enough I had a new notice. I said to the dog, "Great, another asshole has looked at my profile."

Of course, curiosity got the best of me and I looked at this man's profile and saw that his catch.com name was "La Quinta 1625." Why on earth would I be interested in a man from La Quinta, California? That was the last place on the planet I ever wanted to go to again. Then I noticed it said he was a widower. I decided to read his profile to see what he was lying about so that I could report him as a fraud, but it was surprisingly well written. I always look for spelling errors and grammar as a proof of intelligence. This time I couldn't find any mistakes. In fact, even though his location was La Quinta, his profile stated he had another home on Vancouver Island. He actually knew there was a Vancouver Island. I reread his profile and looked at his photos over and over again. I didn't find him all that attractive, but he did golf and I had truly convinced myself that I was looking for a golf partner and not a life partner.

One photo did have me a bit concerned. It was a picture of him and two younger men in a liquor store. The two men were a lot taller than he was, and if they were only 5'8" and 5'10" then he was a troll. There were far too many trolls out there and I didn't want another one of those. There were some other pictures too. One of an old car, which didn't mean anything to me, and a photo of him in a sand trap, so he was telling the truth about being a golfer. Although I did not know it at the time, I can now say that the "old" car was his vintage 1966 Series 1 Jaguar XKE; the sand trap was at St. Andrews in Scotland; the liquor store was actually at Oban, a Scotch distillery in Scotland; and the two taller men were his sons who are 6'1" and 6'4." Hence, he was not a troll.

When you create your internet profile you come up with a fake name and a tag line to follow it. This guy's tag line was, "You never know what tomorrow will bring"; mine was, "Nothing ventured, nothing gained." Because I truly believe in that statement, I decided to send him a note which said, "I'm always looking for a golf partner. Where on the island do you live? I know what you are going through because five years after my husband died, I moved from Winnipeg to the island to begin a new life."

The next morning when he opened his email, he was apparently quite shocked to find a message from me. Rather than going to catch.com and replying from their secure site, he wrote me back from his regular email, breaking all security, and I now knew his name, Douglas John Irving. His name caught me off guard because only thirty-six hours earlier my friend had asked me in a text if I remembered a Barb Irving. I think the universe was announcing his arrival a day before he showed up online.

Within minutes I had his home address and Google-Earthed his house in Courtenay and his house in La Quinta. I lined up the pillars in front of his home with the picture of his old car in front of the house to make sure they matched. I knew what he did for a living and I had his wife's obituary in three newspapers. Nothing was going to get past me.

Doug wrote me back telling me that he was in Vancouver and on his way home to Courtenay and he would contact me from there. I truly wondered if he would keep his word. There was another side of connecting with a man on the internet, any man. If he just joined and was looking for that next stage in his life, he would be blowing through dozens of women, and I wasn't signing up to be one of those.

That night he wrote me a long message from catch.com asking me for my phone number, my email address and permission to call me on Tuesday. We emailed back and forth all evening sharing a bit about ourselves. He even told me he was a member of the Union Club in Victoria and asked if he could take me there for lunch, but the real conversation began at 5 p.m. the next day when he phoned, and we continued to talk every day for the next two weeks.

Doug was in a good position because I was so physically ill that I wasn't as judgmental as I might have been in the past, and I really had nothing better to do than lie on the couch and chat with him every day. I had already made the decision to quit the internet and be happy on my own. This allowed me just to enjoy the moment, and our great conversations made him really grow on me. I looked forward to meeting this man who was so interesting and so very entertaining. Truthfully, his wife had died so recently that I just was being a friendly, compassionate person to chat with. I'd been in his shoes; I just wore higher heels. If he needed a friend, I could be the person who would help him move his life forward; and all I really wanted was a normal guy for the occasional golf game. Besides, he lived two and a half hours away, so the opportunity to see him very often was slim.

Every conversation we had revealed more and more, and I couldn't wait for his call each day. Nine years on the internet and I'd never had conversations like this. At times I felt like I was being interviewed for a job, because his questions were very in depth; he was really investing in me. He in turn, would reveal a lot about himself.

Two questions that really struck me as funny at the time were, "Do you have a double garage?" and "Can you speak Spanish?" I can now say that I really was being interviewed. He's a car guy and needed more garage space to store his vintage cars. And since he doesn't speak Spanish, he was hoping I would be able to converse with his Mexican gardener in La Quinta.

We set up a lunch date for February 7, but I had to cancel because I was still too sick. We set up an alternate date for February 14, Valentine's Day. I felt that was too much of a romance day but didn't dare cancel again or he might think I was a fake. He mentioned that because he would be traveling with his dog he wouldn't be allowed to stay at his club with a pet. I knew he was hinting, so because I had a dog, I told him he was welcome to stay in my guest room. That was where he'd be staying.

On the morning of Tuesday, February 14, 2012 I went back to the clinic and almost tearfully told the doctor that I needed a miracle and a makeover by 4 p.m.

Doug had told me a lot about single malt Scotch, which he loved, so I went to the liquor store and spent $120 on a bottle of Oban and had it waiting for him with a chilled crystal glass on a silver tray with a small ice bucket.

At four thirty that day, Doug walked up my sidewalk. It didn't feel awkward at all because we had talked so often. He came in with this beautiful Siberian husky named Trubbie. Doug had a long-stem red rose for me and a bottle of Glayva, my favorite liqueur, and expressed his approval of the Scotch that was waiting for him.

I offered to take them both upstairs to show him where he'd be staying. On the left was my beautiful office with a Juliette balcony overlooking my courtyard. Doug would be sleeping in my equally beautiful guest room... but when I pointed it out to him, I turned, and my sight line went into my office. There was no way to express my thoughts politely. I screamed, "YOUR DOG IS SHITTING IN MY OFFICE!"

This was Doug's first date in forty-three years and there was his dog shooting diarrhea all over my office, rotating in a circle like a sprinkler system. I wanted to kill them both. Doug turned to me and as the color from his face drained to pale white he said, "Is the first date over?"

I was not happy with Doug's dog Trubbie, whose full name is Trouble. I handed Doug every old towel I could find and had him clean up the mess. In the end I had to have the carpets cleaned. Fortunately, the rest of the date went much better. I can't remember what I ate, and I know we didn't dance, but when we got back to the dogmobile (Doug's oldest car) where we had left Trubbie for the evening, something absolutely magical happened. At some point in our two weeks of conversation he must have asked me my favorite song, because when I buckled up my seatbelt Doug said, "Sit back and relax." He had downloaded not one but four different versions of Van Morrison's "Moon Dance," my song, and I turned my face to the window and the tears simply rolled down my cheeks. The man for me had finally shown up and I knew I had to really pay attention.

Doug lived and worked in the USA and had spent his winters in La Quinta with his wife. Their summers were spent in Courtenay, although Doug was traveling most days. On the Monday of December 12, 2011 Doug was in Houston when he got the call from a friend that his wife had been found in the living room of their California home; she had passed away from a massive heart attack two days earlier, at the age of sixty-one. Christmas was just two weeks away, so the family had planned to gather in the desert to celebrate Doug's own sixty-first birthday on December 23, and to visit for the holidays. Now it was an extremely difficult time for them. On top of it all, on January 5 Doug got a call from one of his neighbors to tell him that smoke was coming out of the house in Courtenay. They had left a housekeeper to tend to the house while they were away for the winter. On that day she put a chicken in a pot to boil and left the house. Although it was a smoke fire and there was no flame damage, the smoke contained chicken fat, and everything had to be removed from the house for cleaning.

Doug needed to head back to Courtenay; but before leaving the desert, his friend Bill, who was also a widower, suggested that at some point he may want to make some changes in his life and to check out catch.com. Bill's sons were on the site and having a great time. On Sunday, January 29, when Doug signed on to catch.com it was purely to see what it was all about. He had absolutely no intention of looking for a date, a partner, or a wife; he was simply curious. The previous day was the Celebration of Life for his wife, Sandi, in Vancouver, and he still had one more to host in Courtenay. Mine was the only profile he looked at or read simply because my photo was nice, and from that he saw that I was a widow. He was not interested in making contact, as it was far too soon. He didn't know that catch.com sent me a notice saying that he had taken a peek and didn't understand how I could send him a note that same day.

Raised in Victoria, Doug is the only one in his family who was not born in Winnipeg. His mother and uncle still live there. When he read my message to him mentioning Winnipeg, he was more impressed with my hometown than my looks or anything my profile stated. He simply wanted to know more, and the conversation started. I now tease him that I had been a widow for twelve years and he a widower for about twelve minutes.

We couldn't believe the life details that we had in common. His late father and his Uncle Bud and I all grew up on the same street and went to the same elementary school. We also had the same family doctor who lived four houses from my grandmother on St. Anthony Street. At the age of eighty-six his uncle, who had been a widower for several years, was marrying his childhood sweetheart, Peg. Peg also went to the same school as I did and grew up about seven houses from my grandmother. His uncle's first marriage and Doug's son's wedding day were on my birthday, and Doug's father and Dennis shared the same birthday. Since 1962 Bud had lived on the same street and ten houses down from my only cousin in Winnipeg. But the biggest surprise of all: my family business in Winnipeg for almost a hundred years was taxidermy, and Doug's family owned a funeral business in Winnipeg that was started in 1879. We joke that we have "dead" covered, and that we are both well preserved. We even figured out that when Dennis's grandfather, who was the chief of Winnipeg Fire Dept #1, died from cancer at an early age, it would have been Doug's great-grandfather who buried him.

I would learn much later why Doug was so anxious to meet me in person. He wasn't too sure I was real and wanted to be certain that I was who I said I was, and not some lonely woman who lived in a three-story walk-up with eight cats. He also chose to take me to the posh Union Club for dinner to be certain that I knew how to properly use a knife and fork. During every conversation he would call me his "Costco." He finally explained that his late wife had a rule: if you saw something at Costco that you liked, don't go home and think about it overnight, because if you go back the next day to get it, it will be gone. Doug was afraid if he waited the appropriate amount of time to meet me, someone would snatch me up and I'd be off the market.

I golfed, drank Scotch and loved football. To him I was the perfect woman. Little did he know I'd been waiting twelve years, somewhat impatiently, for him to show up.

The day following our first date Doug gave me a tour of his Victoria—all the houses he'd lived in growing up, and the schools he attended. We walked Ogden Point to the lighthouse, one of my favorite places, and that's where he surprised me with a kiss. I cooked dinner at home that evening. Doug had brought lots of DVD concerts to watch, because the following day, I really had to rest.

We went out for dinner that night and after we got home, I told him there was something I wanted to share with him: I read him the first and only chapter of this book. While reading, I was stopped dead in my tracks. It was now Thursday, February 16. I had discovered that Dennis was an addict on Thursday, February 16, seventeen years earlier.

Doug came for a visit the next weekend and my mom got to meet him. Trubbie had his diarrhea again, but this time on my hardwood floors... and that's how I got my first two dozen long-stemmed roses. On the third week we golfed and went out to dinner. Trubbie had a third accident, again on my carpets, and this time Doug bought me a Bissell green machine carpet cleaner. After that Trubbie was no trouble at all.

It's difficult to describe Doug, as there are too many superlatives for one book. He is everything on my Top 10 list. I wanted someone who was a football fan, and I got a touchdown with this football family. His uncle played in the Canadian Football League and was a referee in the CFL as well. Doug coached football and both he and his sons played. His youngest son went to university on a football scholarship. I'm now part of Doug's international NFL football pool among friends and family in Canada and the US, and too many times the grandchildren win the pool. He's a tall enough golfer, has his own lunch money, loves to travel, and has a head of hair that he'll never lose. He got bonus points for having been in a band as a teen, which is very cool in my books. I saw a picture him at sixteen, and how I wish we'd met back in the '60s. I had hoped for a partner who would cook alongside me, but I changed my mind. I can whip up a meal by myself; but Doug is a really good dancer and I can't dance alone. During our courtship—and he really did court me—every time I saw him, he had eighteen long-stem roses for me. Over time I must have had seventy dozen roses. My mom and I were convinced that because he had been in the funeral business, he must have gotten a big discount on flowers somewhere. He is handsome and handy and without a doubt he always has my back.

It was finally time for me to drive up to Courtenay to see where he lived. I took my mom with me. The seniors' resort where she lived also had a location up island and she could stay there for free. Her dear lifelong friend Pat lived there as well.

Doug told me he had quite an art collection, so my request was to be met at his front door with a chilled glass of Sauvignon blanc so that I could have an art tour first. As we walked through the dining room I turned around and looked at the table and gasped. He had set the table with bone china, crystal champagne flutes and silver flatware, which turned out to be the same silver pattern I had. He even used charger plates. There was a bouquet of red roses in the center. What man does that? I looked at him in dismay and threw my arms around him with my eyes filled with joyful tears. That's what I'd been missing... a man with class. The starter was shrimp cocktail, with the appropriate cocktail glassware filled with crushed ice. The main course, which we agreed he would never make again, got an A+ for effort and he bought a cheesecake for dessert. I was absolutely smitten and over the moon.

Three months earlier on Saturday, December 10, 2011, it was no coincidence that I was on that airplane flying back from Cabo San Lucas when the pilot told us if we looked out the right side of the aircraft, we would see La Quinta, CA. At that precise hour, between 7 and 8 p.m. Doug's wife Sandi died in La Quinta, right below me. I like to think that as her spirit left this earth, she saw me, sad and feeling completely alone in this world, and said, "There's the perfect woman for my Doug."

# 49 – Audrey Isabella

Audrey Isabella Edwards was my mother, and the best mom a girl could ever have. She was also an emotionally controlled and abused wife. She hid that fact from me until I was grown up and had been married. She needed to protect me and didn't want to turn me against my dad. They fought often and it really upset me when I was very young. When my dad threw his salad at the rec room wall and the thousand island dressing glued the lettuce to the wood paneling, Mom refused to clean up the mess he made. It stayed there for weeks. I thought that was normal. When you're an only child there's no one to talk to.

In her mid-seventies Mom had a terrible time with her voice. She would go to speak, and nothing would come out. She saw many doctors over the years who wanted to inject her with Botox, but I begged her to hold off. Once my parents had retired and moved west, my father's control was almost unbearable for Mom, but she did not have the courage to leave until July 1998. He monitored her every move, and for fifty-six years he had made her take her measurements each month and record them to prove she wasn't gaining weight. As a result, she became obsessed with my weight and everyone else's. Once my dad took his life, her life changed for the better, and it wasn't long until her voice became strong again. The fear that had controlled her had also controlled her voice.

On the first anniversary of my dad's death, Mom and I took a two-week bus trip in Italy and a Mediterranean cruise. Then two years later it was the first anniversary of Dennis's death, and we took a three-week cruise to the Baltic. Our trips would continue, as we traveled very well together. There was only one problem. My dad had convinced her that packing a suitcase properly was more important than the vacation itself. For weeks before we left, she would stress obsessively, and on occasion break down in tears, fearing her suitcase was not packed right. I had a very difficult time convincing her that it didn't matter; and for the trip home it would start all over again.

The fear of not doing things perfectly never went away. She needed to feel free and independent. I wanted that for her too, but once into her late '80s when she really did need assistance, it could become a battle of wills because she thought I was trying to control her just like Dad. In 2005 I moved to Victoria and into my new and beautiful home. Shortly after I arrived, I was told they were building a senior's "resort" at the top of my street. My mom and I hadn't lived in the same city since 1975, so I approached her about a move, and it was an instant "yes." In June of 2008 I packed up her condo in Kelowna and brought her back to Victoria in time for the opening of her newly completed home. It would turn out to be the best decision we ever made. Time spent with someone you love and the memories you create together last forever, and we had so much fun sharing.

August 27, 2011 was my mom's ninetieth birthday. She was pretty feisty even at ninety. For her seventy-fifth birthday I'd taken her hot air ballooning over Calgary, and for her eightieth we went whitewater rafting in class-four rapids in Denali, Alaska. She wanted to top that for her ninetieth birthday. Since US President George Bush Sr. had parachuted out of an airplane, she decided that was what she would do. Her doctor said, "No way," so she made me take her to another doctor for a second opinion and he said, "Absolutely no way." That's when I had the opportunity to hire a pilot and charter a plane to take us flying on the morning of her birthday. It was a total surprise and she said it was the best day of her life! My mom had dreamed of being a pilot since her brother was killed in a Spitfire in the Battle of Britain. We had a very young female pilot who was brought to tears when we told her just how important this flight was. Mom got to take control of the plane for a very short time. We went to her favorite restaurant for lunch, then celebrated again at dinner, followed by a party and birthday cake for her at her complex. My six dear friends who had helped me with her over the years came to celebrate as well.

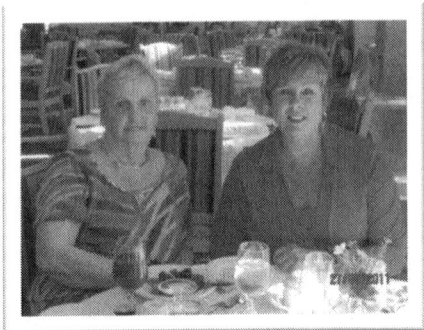

In February of 2012 when I met Doug, Mom was all ears when it came to learning about this new man. Of course, she was a skeptic because I hadn't had much luck in the past. But she was the first person I introduced him to, and she liked him immediately. I am so happy that she got to meet him and to know him. She even got to see the home that I would eventually live in with him. Doug and I celebrated her ninety-first birthday together. I still have a photo of her on my desk taken that day. She was having a glass of white wine and staring out at the ocean. She told me she didn't want to live to see her ninety-second. She was happy because she knew that I was happy, and she told me she was ready to go.

A month later she was in the hospital. My mom had more bumps and falls in her life than I can count, and each time she would bang her head. Over time it resulted in fluid on the brain and even though she had a shunt to help, her problems continued. This time she was in the hospital four weeks. Then she was moved from independent living to a care ward at her resident facility, where she still had her own beautiful room with her own furniture.

She was absolutely thrilled with her new accommodations, and Doug and I celebrated with her at the Christmas party that year. I could see changes in her, and I was beginning to get worried. Doug had invited me to spend the winter with him in La Quinta and I was afraid to leave her. Of course, she insisted that I go, she was fine and had lots of care. I would later learn that she phoned Doug to find out what his intentions were. She wanted to be sure he would be there for me and take care of me when she was gone. That's truly the definition of a mother's love.

I will never forget that Christmas, my last with her. We went out for a wonderful dinner on the twenty-fourth and drove around to look at all the Christmas lights. We had Christmas dinner together at her place. Boxing Day morning we planned to have breakfast, and then the dog and I were taking the ferry to Vancouver. Doug was spending Christmas with his children there and it would be the first time I was meeting them. I had been stewing for weeks about how I would react on the morning of December 26, because I had a terrible feeling it would be the last time Mom and I would be together. She had even given me the ring she wore every day, the one we designed together when Dad died. She wanted me to have possession of it in case something happened to her.

Doug and I arrived in La Quinta on Friday, December 28, spent our first New Year's Eve together, and were looking forward to a new beginning for both of us. On Wednesday, January 2, 2013 I got a phone call while I was sitting at the pool. Nursing staff had found my mom unconscious on the floor and an ambulance had been called. I was told the end was near and to book a flight home. I arrived back in Victoria at midnight and went straight to the hospital. Mom had a brain hemorrhage which blinded her, and she was in and out of consciousness. Over the next few days, although she knew I was there, she was rarely conscious and could barely speak. She had made a living will and did not want any extraordinary measures taken to keep her alive. This was her time and what she wanted.

She did speak three times, once she knew I was there. Although it took a great deal of difficulty, she told me, "Go back, go back, Doug, Doug." She knew I had found happiness, and that's where she wanted me to be, with Doug. A week later, she was still with me and managed to say, "Look, there's my mother in a chair." Often people in their last days will claim they saw a relative who's already passed. Dennis told us he'd seen his cousin Clifford. Sitting in a chair was all I ever saw my late Grandma Edwards do. She was very large and had mental health issues and just sat around all day and all night. There was an empty chair by the wall in Mom's room, so it seemed very possible that Mom saw her own mother (who had come for her), sitting down. Had she said, "My mom's standing here," I wouldn't have believed her.

The next day Mom was moved to a private room. There was just her and me together counting down the minutes of her life. Her heart was very strong. She held on until the evening of Saturday, January 12, and she had one more thing to say because she saw something incredible. Deaf in both ears and blinded by multiple brain hemorrhages, having been in and out of a coma for ten days, she sat bolt upright and in the strongest voice I'd ever heard out of her she said, "You have got to be kidding!"

## 50 – She Sells Real Estate from the Other Side

June 8, 2013, one day before my birthday, I was sound asleep at my daughter's home when I was suddenly awakened with an overwhelming urge to look at real estate online. That was just plain weird because the thought came to me in my sleep as if in a dream. And not just homes anywhere and everywhere, but a house in the complex where Doug had his vacation home, in La Quinta, CA. I had no idea why I felt that I needed to do a search, but within minutes I found a home on the lake that really caught my eye. This started as a joke because later in the day, when I talked to Doug, I told him that I had found a house for myself five doors from his and that if I bought it, he wouldn't have to walk home very far every night.

I now think Mom sent me that little push as a birthday gift, because the idea of me buying a home in Southern California, a thought that I had never, ever considered, was suddenly becoming a reality. Doug and I were spending most of our time together, and although he had a very nice home, it was where his wife Sandi passed away, so I was never completely comfortable there. Suddenly the conversation became serious and when I returned home, we discussed it and I put an offer on the lake house with fingers crossed. The deal went through, and I was ecstatic. The house was beautiful but unloved and would require a three-month renovation, so I had to get to Southern California ASAP.

Back in January of 2009 I had made my first trip to La Quinta with Bill Badman and swore I would never go back there. Now I not only owned a home in La Quinta, but every time I walked out my new front door I looked up at the side of a mountain. It was the same mountain I'd spent a week staring at with Mr. Badman, only from the other side. I didn't know it, but that trip was a glimpse into my future. My life would be only a stone's throw from where all of that terrible week occurred. To me this was destiny.

It was now the third week in June, and I had the huge challenge of selling my home in Victoria. It was a perfect house and needed no repairs. It was decorated beautifully and didn't even need staging. I was thrilled when I had three showings the first week, but my heart sank when my agent told me that there would have been three offers in a row if there had only been a parking spot for a second car. There were nine town homes in my development, and I was the only one with a single garage with no additional parking for guests. Without my knowledge my agent's partner phoned our strata president and asked if I could add paving stones to my sidewalk and make a guest parking spot like all my neighbors had. That request, although it did not come from me, sparked WWIII with the strata.

I had some other obstacles in front of me. I was taking possession of the house in California on October 1. I had to be there to get the renovation started so it could be completed by January 1, because we had rented out Doug's home for the first of the year. That meant my house in Victoria had be sold ASAP and packed up completely, the contents divided by the third week of September. A lot of things would be moved up to Courtenay to Doug's house, and the remainder that was going to the USA had be listed for US Customs. I was told I didn't have to actually count the silverware, but I had to account for every single possession. By the time everything was packed up I had a huge binder, having written down and numbered everything I owned.

Second complication, August 7, Doug and I were to fly to Dublin, Ireland for a month of sightseeing and golf. August in Ireland is a very wet month and most of our games would be on foot because they rarely use carts on links courses. This would take more energy on my part than I could imagine. Having always dreamed of seeing Ireland, we both decided this was the best way to test our relationship. The trip was planned long before any notion of selling my home. This test could have been the end of us, so it was quite a gamble. But it was the best trip ever, and it cemented our relationship for life.

Third complication, Doug had offered up the use of his home in Courtenay for a fundraiser at his old high school earlier that spring. It was a silent auction item, and the prize was a weekend of "Golf and

Gourmet" on July 11. Doug would be paying for the golf and I was to be the gourmet cook. This was something we'd been excited about for months, but now I was trying to sell my house under extreme pressure from the strata council in my development (though they wouldn't budge on the parking spot), and I was having difficulty focusing on the weekend at hand. That day, in a wee bit of desperation, I stood in Doug's back yard and offered up a prayer and a plea: "Mom, you know I never give up, but I'm not going to win this battle. Do I just cave in and forget it or do I keep on fighting for another parking spot? Please send me a sign."

Within the hour our house guests arrived. I had never met them, and I didn't even know their last names. While getting the appetizers ready to take out to the patio, I chatted with Lisa, our guest. I told her I didn't really know my way around this particular kitchen, as I hadn't made it mine yet. "I'm in the process of moving up here and my house in Victoria is for sale." Lisa just happened to be one of 1200 real estate agents in Victoria and she asked me where my house was. Then she added, "That's a beautiful home and I showed it to Jan's sister last week, but she couldn't put in an offer because there was parking for only one car." ARE YOU KIDDING! The sign I asked for was now received. Thank you, Mom. I may not win but I will never give up the fight.

On August 7 we flew first class from Vancouver to Dublin with my house still unsold. I had a pedicure, and my toes were painted green for the luck of the Irish because I needed all the help I could get, but I still had one more request. While waiting in the Nanaimo ferry parking lot, I once again offered up a prayer and a plea to my mom. Through the car windshield and up towards heaven I said, "Mom please sell my house while we're gone. It has to go, or we won't be able to pack it up and be in La Quinta by the first of October, and the stress of all this will kill my golf games in Ireland." Half kidding, half serious, did I believe she heard me? Not really, but it's fun to never stop wishing, hoping and praying.

After flying all night, we arrived in Frankfurt to change planes. While waiting in the lounge I opened my iPad to check on emails and there was one from my real estate agent, Jean. I had an offer. Gobsmacked doesn't even begin to describe how I felt. There were conditions on the offer, but I didn't care. I accepted whatever they wanted. Twin sisters from another province, they had two homes that needed to be sold. Not a problem. I'd do anything for them because they only needed one parking spot.

The next three weeks of Irish golfing heaven flew by and our trip was sadly beginning to wind down. We had one more stop on Louge Eske in Donegal at the beautiful and incredibly romantic Harvey's Point. On our last morning there I had an email from my real estate agent reminding me that even though I had a conditional offer, if I lowered the price a bit, I could still attract more interested parties, so I lowered the price. On our last evening we had a spectacular dinner and raised our glasses in a toast to my mom for finding me a buyer. Once back in our room I checked my emails and there was a photo that had me almost drop to the floor. The ladies who had a conditional offer must have seen that I lowered the price and because they didn't want to lose my house, they removed all conditions. There was a photo of my agent under a SOLD sign. What a perfect day. It was August 27, 2013 and it would have been my mom's ninety-second birthday. Thanks, Mom. I love you like crazy.

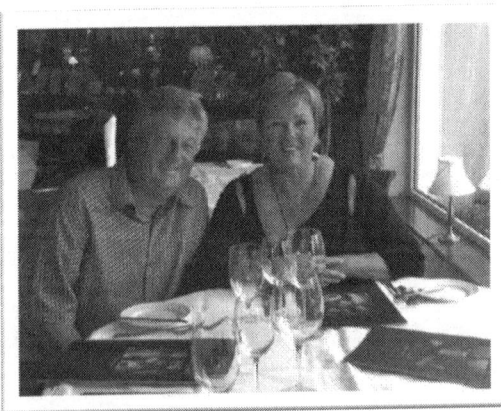

One down, two to go...

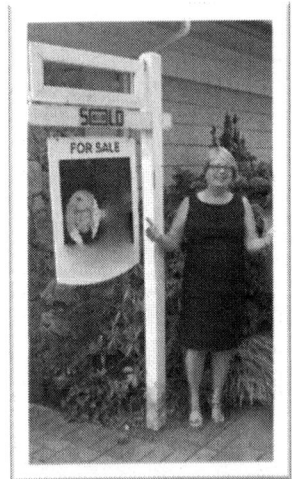

By the spring of 2015 Doug and I realized that three houses were at least one house too many, and we decided to put his house in La Quinta on the market in April. It was the spring of lots of showings and the summer of no offers. Very stressful. We just didn't know what to do, and after five months it was very difficult to be patient.

We decided to take another trip, and on September 15 we left for a golf game and a few days in Whistler, BC, followed by a cruise to Alaska for a week. We'd been in this jam before, so once again, while waiting for the ferry in Nanaimo I decided it was time for a chat with my mom. For a second time, through the windshield of the car, I offered up a plea: "Please, Mom, can you do it again? We really need Doug's house to sell" Ha, ha, giggle, giggle.

We did not take this request too seriously, thinking that the sale of my house two years before had been a bit of a fluke. Literally four days later, as we were walking up the gangplank of the ship, where the sign clearly says, "No cell phones," Doug's cell phone rang. It was his real estate agent in La Quinta with the news that he had an offer on his house.

A happy and exciting time aboard the cruise ship became very challenging because of communications when cruising, but Doug didn't care. He spent many a morning back and forth from our stateroom to the purser's office getting documents printed and scanned. We didn't care, it was SOLD.

Last, but certainly not least...

They say things come in threes, and by the spring of 2017 I had made the decision to sell my home on the lake in La Quinta. It was really my little dream house. Perfect in every way. The décor, view of the mountains and lake were breathtaking, and it was really wonderful... until it wasn't. Still it was difficult to give it up. The Canadian dollar had dropped dramatically since I bought the house, and as Canadians we could only be there six months out of the year; so the monthly cost to me was extensive.

We listed it in February and had an open house by an agent every Saturday until the end of March, when we hosted them ourselves.

We flew back to Canada at the end of April with it still not sold. On the May 24 long weekend, we headed off to Vancouver, and on the way to the ferry in Nanaimo I said to Doug, "Remind me to have another real estate chat with my mom." Well, we forgot. We had a list of things to do in Vancouver because we were starting a big reno on our house in Courtenay on July 1 and there was a long list of shopping to be done. Halfway across the Strait of Georgia I remembered that I hadn't put in my request with Mom. In a panic but with another big giggle I hollered through the front window of the car and over the roar of the engines, telling Doug that she would never hear me through all the steel structure that holds a ferry together.

We went right to King of Floors to look at hardwood floors. While standing there with the company owner, my cell phone rang... and you guessed it. It was my real estate agent in La Quinta with an offer, an excellent one. The third time was the charm.

That may have been the end of my mom's real estate ventures, but something else happened along the way.

My son and I had a very close relationship for the first twenty-five years of his life. Then his dad died, and although all of our lives changed, his changed the most. He lost his youth and what was supposed to be the best time in his life, because he had to take over the family business. Not by choice but probably more out of guilt. Not only was it owned by his father before him, but also his grandfather and his great-grandfather. Not many family businesses make it to a fourth generation, and he felt obligated to carry on tradition. In 2003 his sister moved west and in 2005 I moved to Victoria, leaving him behind to slay the dragons and defend the castle. In 2008 it was just the two of us against the world, shutting down the business, closing the doors and walking away. I had hoped and prayed that year-long test we lived through would help us bond and be close once more. But it didn't.

Nothing changed until the spring of 2012 when Doug was a new part of my life and Damien (with his girlfriend at the time) planned a trip to Victoria. The two men in my life would meet. I understand that Damien's sister even warned him to "be nice" because Doug sounded like a keeper. Dinner that evening was really fun I made a family favorite, prime rib and Yorkshire pudding, as well as Damien's favorite fruit trifle for dessert. I could clearly see they were having a great time together. Doug's two sons are the same age as Damien, and Doug was a businessman, so they had a lot to talk about while they drank Scotch.

The next morning, following breakfast, Doug drove home, and Damien called me out to the patio to talk. He was full of questions about Doug. He fired one after another at me for fifteen to twenty minutes, then he stopped and sank back into his chair. A single tear rolled down his cheek and he said, "Dad would really like that man." There it was. The ice was forever broken. My son had always said he wanted me to date and hoped that I would find happiness, but he never wanted to meet anyone I was seeing or even hear about them. Of course, he never knew about my horrific dating history. In the beginning if I brought up the subject of even having coffee with a man, he would cover his ears and go, "la, la, la" like a kid. There are far too many "not so good" men out there and he didn't want his mother to be "taken." Now he could clearly see I'd met a really good man and he was very interested in having Doug in all of our lives. He knew his dad would approve.

For my entire life my mother reminded me that when she cut her wedding cake, she wished for seven little boys and she only got one daughter. So, my Damien was the light of her life. In March of 2014 Damien paid his first visit to the desert and spent a wonderful week with Doug and me. It was like having a brand-new relationship with my son. This gave my mom one more opportunity to give me a message. Early the next morning, while I was still in bed, lying on my left side, I felt a hug from behind and a kiss on my neck behind my right ear. I thought it was Doug, but I could hear him in our closet getting dressed for his early morning walk. I tried to call out but could neither move nor speak. I was totally immobile. This had happened to me before, in February of 2008, when I swear Dennis kissed me. But this time it felt different. This wasn't a kiss from a husband. This wasn't the feeling of "I'm sorry." I knew as only a daughter would know, that hug and kiss came from my mom. She'd been watching and listening the evening before, and she knew that now all wounds had been healed and we'd been able to put all the past behind us.

I was really surprised when one more thing happened on August 27, 2016, on what would have been Mom's ninety-fifth birthday. Doug and I were golfing in Vancouver. It was a links course very close to the ocean. As we approached a par 3 over a lake, I thought it would be an excellent way to celebrate her ninety-fifth, so I offered up a prayer and plea for a birdie, but my ball went straight into the water and was lost forever. Would you believe, at the very next hole Doug and I both got birdies. My mom loved her golf, and she was really good at it, so it was the perfect way to acknowledge her special day. She was happiest when she was golfing, and she knew I was too.

# 51 – It's not a Pebble, it's a Rock

Pebble Beach Golf Course, just south of San Francisco on the Monterey Peninsula, has been on my bucket list for years. The odds of me ever golfing there are slim to none. I am certainly not a good enough golfer to play there and the price is a little too steep for my wallet. I'm a very average golfer with a high handicap. I think I started golfing a little too late in life to ever be really good. I have no natural athletic ability, but I don't embarrass myself. I always look good, because it's all about the outfit. I absolutely love the game and I continue to dream big.

It was mid-November 2014, and we were all packed to head south for the winter—Doug and I plus one Siberian husky and one Bichon, in the dogmobile. We were so loaded for a winter in Southern California that we resembled the Beverly Hillbillies.

Interstate 5, which runs from the Canadian border the length of Washington, Oregon and California, is not one of my favorite drives. Boring is an understatement, so this trip Doug decided to take an extra day and a more scenic route. On day two we left Medford, Oregon in the rain and headed to the Monterey Peninsula.

Doug really wanted me to see Pebble Beach. He'd yet to golf there and knew it was a big item on my bucket list. As we approached the peninsula the clouds cleared, and we were surrounded by blue sky and beautiful sunshine. We had a reservation at a cute boutique hotel in Carmel, so we took a short drive around first and then headed to the golf course. Upon arriving in the parking lot, we first had to walk the dogs. When I got out of the car the air was filled with the smell of money and I felt like a bum. I was covered in dog hair and my hair and makeup had been done at 6 a.m. I was pretty faded looking.

We first checked out the pro shop. I wanted a small souvenir, preferably something with a bit of bling. When I saw the prices, I gasped and settled on a sparkly ball marker and a Pebble Beach towel. No $85 Pebble Beach visor for me. Doug wanted to walk through the lodge and out to the eighteenth green. The vista was spectacular, and we paused to take a few pictures. We had a few minutes to enjoy the view, so Doug suggested we take a seat on the bench to rest and take it all in. As I walked up to the bench my cell phone rang but there was no one there. It struck me as strange because I had just put my US SIM card into my phone. My ring tone is "our" "Moon Dance" song by Van Morrison. As I sat down, I saw that Doug was turning around. He was stooped over and was headed for the ground. My heart stopped. At our age that can happen a lot, but Doug just dropped to one knee and suddenly I was the one having the heart attack. Pebble Beach, eighteenth green... Location, location, location!

I was the one from the very beginning of our relationship to loudly proclaim, "I'll never get married again." I stuck to my guns and we didn't bring it up, but over the summer of 2014 I had softened, and Doug and I had decided we were ready. It was time. We had seventy-three years of marriage between us, so we knew how to do this, and we never wanted to be apart.

I can't say that I didn't know an engagement was coming, but I certainly didn't think it would be that day, November 19, 2014. Both of my children were coming to visit us in the desert for Christmas and it would be my first Christmas with both of them in fifteen years. Christmas morning would have been the perfect time for a proposal. There was also the anniversary of our first date on Valentine's Day. I really was completely caught off guard by a proposal on this particular day at Pebble Beach.

Doug's mouth was moving but all I could hear was a ringing in my ears. Then he pulled out the ring. An unbelievable three-carat diamond solitaire with four channeled diamonds on each side. This was no pebble; it was a rock. The ring wouldn't fit because I was so swollen from traveling. I couldn't stop bawling but I must have said "yes."

The bartender was thrilled and told everyone in the bar that Doug had just popped the question. As it turned out, Doug had put the ring in his pocket just that morning. At that point he wasn't sure if the location would work out. What he did try to figure out was how to get someone to play "our song" when he proposed. Was my cell phone call simply a coincidence? I think not. Once again, all the stars above were in perfect alignment for us. I have now taken Pebble Beach off my bucket list. Eighteen holes would pale in comparison to my hole in one at the bench.

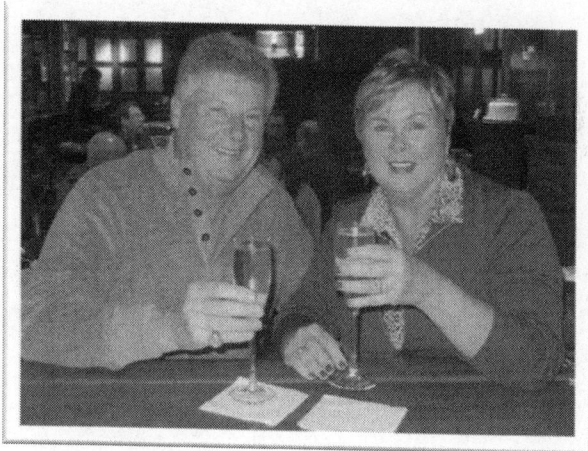

## 52 – Grandpa and Grandma Get Married

How do you plan a wedding at our age? Doug was married in 1970 and I was married in 1971. We had work to do, and the first thing would be to pick a date and a location. It was now January 2015, so to start with, we picked January 3, 2016, one year away

For the location, why not our own back yard at our home in Courtenay, BC? Not the yard, exactly, but the golf course. We live on the eighth fairway at Crown Isle Resort. It's beautiful and we are both members. They have a lovely gazebo and we've seen many weddings there before.

Realizing we weren't kids anymore, we thought maybe we should make it sooner rather than later. We wanted to be sure that we'd still be around, so we looked for an earlier date. I phoned my oldest granddaughter Ella and asked permission to be married on her eighth birthday, and to also ask her to be a flower girl. So, Sunday, August 2, 2015 it would be.

We had decisions to make. Top of the list, the bride needed a dress. I went looking for dresses in Palm Springs, but two wedding shops had been closed. No one gets married there, just divorced. I couldn't find anything that would work. We would have to make some decisions from afar; and at first, I didn't have a clue how we would do it. Then I remembered that when I spoke with my dentist in September, he told me he'd just been married at Crown Isle. I phoned him and asked if I could give his wife a call—the joy of living in a small town! A phone call later I had the wedding planner, florist, names for photographers, and where I should get the cake.

Now for the enormous decision of "how big do we go"? That was a tough one because we both have wonderful friends and family on Vancouver Island and across the country. But I wanted this wedding to be all about family. Between us, Doug and I have a total of six grandchildren, four granddaughters and two grandsons between the ages of six and ten. I wanted our wedding to be all about them and the joining of our two families, because our children had never met. Additionally, if and when our grandchildren wanted to move in with their boyfriend or girlfriend, I didn't want them to say, "Why can't we? Grandma is living with her boyfriend…" I really felt that we had to set an example.

The decision was made. Only our children and grandchildren would be invited to the ceremony and reception. Then we extended an invitation to our relatives, neighbors and friends in town, to join us for the nuptials and a glass of champagne during the "toasts." Following that, the family would gather for a private celebration in the Silver Room at the clubhouse for dinner and dancing.

While still in California we ordered the girls' dresses and shopped for the boys' outfits and accessories. Such fun. Doug's oldest granddaughter would be the junior bridesmaid, and there would be three flower girls. Both our grandsons would carry the rings, a task they took very seriously on our wedding day. I wanted my dress and all of the accessories to be in my possession by the time we left for home. After only two tries I found the perfect dress online at Macy's. It was exactly what I had in mind. I wished I could walk down the aisle with the price tag still on, as it was only $29 more than my wedding dress in 1971. Oh, how I love a bargain.

We didn't have to worry about what Doug would wear because he already had a tuxedo that fit him perfectly. We decided against the formal bow tie and cummerbund. Doug had literally dozens of ties so in early May, together we picked one that was black with a charcoal sparkly stripe and set it aside. Very classy indeed.

We hit the ground running when we arrived home. With the help of a wedding planner the ballroom would be an explosion of pink. The best idea I had was to have a pink wedding themed gift bag as the centerpiece on the "kids table." Inside they would find a new box of 800 pieces of Lego. Grandma knows best. Doug picked the cake. It had to be lemon with a ton of butter cream icing, and we ordered a cake topper that we could keep forever. We made plane reservations and sent out or hand-delivered invitations to our friends and neighbors.

We treated our wedding the same as we would have if five hundred were attending. We carefully planned the menu, which Doug printed out beautifully along with place cards. We bought Roger's Chocolates, which originate from Vancouver Island, for each adult, and happy-face chocolate suckers for the kids, all wrapped in pink.

One night while we were at a local pub, we heard a pianist and I mentioned to Doug how great it would be to have live music. He said, "Why not?" and the pianist agreed to play for us. I wanted to pick the music, because next to my dress that was the most important element of the wedding for me. Doug would walk down to "Feeling Good," Michael Buble's version, and of course I would walk down that aisle, for the last time in my life, to "At Last." No song ever was more appropriate.

Doug and I made the decision to move into the resort on the Friday night of our wedding weekend to give our family of thirteen time to bond as they all stayed in the house. We certainly had the room, and I know all the grandkids were excited about meeting and gaining new cousins. All but one would be there by Friday. I had the meals planned and the agenda set.

Saturday morning all the girls went to a local festival in town while all the boys went golfing. In the afternoon I treated the big girls to manicures and pedicures, and for dinner we had a "Prairie Meets West Coast" formal family dinner: British Columbia halibut on a bed of Manitoba wild rice. There was Nanaimo bar cheesecake for dessert, of course.

After a wonderful evening Doug and I stumbled across two fairways in the dark, back to the resort and our suite, hardly able to believe that in less than twenty-four hours we would be husband and wife.

## 53 – My Happily Ever After Chapter

I've always been a bit superstitious, and my wedding day was no exception. After coming this far I wasn't willing to risk anything. When I rolled over early on the morning of Sunday, August 2, 2015, I did not want Doug and me to see each other. I hid my head under the covers while he slipped out of bed for another golf game with the boys. He would stay at the house until the magic hour and I had the entire day to get ready.

I've never had seven hours to get ready for an event. I just sat and thought about my journey. And, what a journey it had been. I learned so many lessons, but mostly I learned about myself. I have gone through life acting as if I was a strong and confident woman, and that's how people see me, but I am not. I really had to push myself at every turn. I convinced myself to act as if I could do things, and then I could. Just the move alone in 2005 was enough to shake me in my high heels. That was a huge risk, to sell everything, leave my home and everything behind to start a new life at the age of fifty-five. Looking back, my new life had another strange coincidence. Geoff Smith was the first man I had really connected with on the internet back in 2004. I see that point as the beginning of the changes in my life. We still remain friends. I see my life as having come full circle since that time. By marrying Doug, I would have a new family and Doug's sister had married a Geoff Smith. Doug and I almost fell over when we figured out that one. To me that signaled the end of my journey.

For someone who is known to be very impatient, I certainly took my time finding Mr. Right. But then, I was never looking for Mr. Right Now. My foray into the internet and dating world was about finding someone who was not perfect, but perfect for me. I was never going to lower my standards. I held out for the best and that is what I found. I was also brave in other areas of my life. I traveled, often alone, which is no fun ever. I tried new things, I pushed my boundaries and stepped out of my comfort zone more times than I could count. I became a joiner because you simply can't spend your life sitting home alone. I lost people in my life whom I loved but I found new loves and better friendships. Now here I was having been a widow for fifteen years, I had just turned sixty-five, and I was about to marry the man of my dreams. Even if it did take twelve years for him to show up, I never really gave up hope that "he" was out there. Prince Charming exists and I found him. It was all going to be a very surreal day. I wanted to slow time down and breathe it all in.

My daughter brought the four flower girls to my suite two at a time for manicures and pedicures. They were so cute and so excited. Of course, all of us had our nails done in pink. My heart was already pounding, and it was only 2 p.m.

Back at the house the boys were all partying, but I wouldn't learn that until much later. Our photographer arrived three hours before the wedding to take photos. The men hadn't begun to get ready, but then again, it only takes a man fifteen minutes to look his best.

By 3 p.m. the second photographer arrived at my suite. The girls were all dressed and looked absolutely darling. I was thrilled with their dresses. They were perfect for a golf course wedding. I did my own hair and makeup and was pleased how they both turned out. I couldn't have a bad hair day, not today. I admit to having a two-hour full-blown Bridezilla moment a week before, over my dress. I was never happy with the fit, but it was too late now.

My daughter-in-law Tara brought the little boys over and they were perfect in their pink polo shirts and tan shorts. Time for more photos.

Doug and I had set up a signal. This was important. He would text when he was leaving the house so that I could time my walk from the suite. Of course, he forgot. Then I realized that the boys weren't wearing their boutonnieres. That would mean that Doug didn't have his either. What would a wedding be without a few small glitches? We began our slow walk to the clubhouse while new daughter-in-law Tara raced back home for the flowers.

The ceremony was set for 5 p.m. We arrived at the clubhouse through the main door. I couldn't help but recall that six years earlier one of my girlfriends and I came up to Courtenay to stay at the resort and golf. I had walked through those doors as a hotel guest, never dreaming that someday I would be getting married there and move to live there with the incredible man who would be my husband.

I could see Doug in the distance while his son pinned on his boutonniere, and it stirred up my butterflies. The girls were so excited, and the boys were so serious about their task of carrying the rings. Adorable. Even my daughter, who is one of the calmest persons I know, got super excited realizing that her mother was about be married. She certainly could appreciate what I had gone through to get to this point.

But now for the magic!

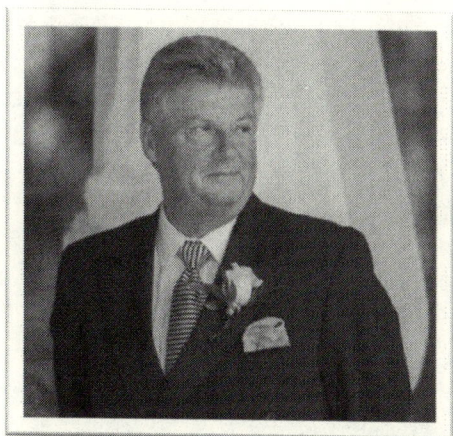

I could hear "Feeling Good," which was Doug's cue to start walking, but I couldn't see him from my vantage point behind a pole. I now know what the expression "all atwitter" means. Every cell in my body was vibrating, certainly not with nerves or fear, but with joy. I do not remember hearing my music to walk to. There was that ringing in my ears again. I warned Doug that I would make him cry, and he brushed many a tear away. We wrote our own vows. Quite simple, but I remember one thing in particular that Doug mentioned that made me laugh. He loves the fact that I am always "matchy, matchy." Having spent many years in fashion I am very particular. The last laugh was on both of us. In May when we decided to select Doug's tie and set it aside with his tux, we were both confident we had made the right choice. As I approached this handsome man waiting to make me his, all I could see was a navy blue and silver tie. Sixty-five-year-old eyes had made the wrong decision, as it wasn't black and silver after all.

How I wished my mom could have lived long enough to see this day. She was overjoyed that I had met Doug but knew we weren't talking about marriage at that time. I did have someone there who was indeed a wonderful substitute. My mom's best friend of over eighty years came to our wedding. Pat has known me even before I was born. She and her family had always been a big part of my life growing up. Pat was at my wedding in 1971 and hosted a bridal shower for me at the time. I could see her in a big white sunhat as I walked down the aisle. She was ninety-two years young and I blew her a kiss as I walked by. It truly meant the world to me to have her there. We also planned a little surprise for everyone and had a rehearsal with all the kids the evening before. I popped gummy bears in their mouths so they wouldn't talk and would listen to what grandma was saying. At the beginning of our ceremony, we had the Marriage Commissioner read a passage we'd written about the role of a grandparent. Then we asked the six grandkids to take a vow accepting us as their grandparents, and we took a vow to take all of them as our grandchildren. A very special moment truly joining the two families together.

The ceremony was over all too quickly. Hugs and kisses and congratulations all around. We wanted everyone in our family to be a part of our day, so Doug's oldest son, DJ, and my daughter, Keele, signed the register with us, and Doug's son AJ gave the toast to the happy couple. Still a traditionalist, I wanted a "toast to the bride" and asked my son Damien if he would do the honors. In his speech he said,

"My mom has been through an awful lot since my dad died, so Dad looked down from heaven and hand-picked Doug for her." Perfect.

Even I was stunned when we walked into the ballroom an hour later. It really was an explosion of pink, so beautiful and full of bling. The candles, which were already lit, smelled like fresh strawberries. The giant bag of Lego was a huge hit for the kids and was dumped on the floor immediately. That would keep all the kids busy while we had more champagne and appetizers. The meal was fabulous, and we kept the wine flowing. Doug had spent hours downloading music for dancing, but only the kids got on the dance floor.

We did all the things you'd expect at a larger reception. Doug and I had our "first" dance to The Bee Gee's "Wedding Day," one of my favorites. We never did get to dance to "Moon Dance" as I had hoped, but then that song had already played a major role in our relationship.

Our grandchildren got a real kick out of tossing the garter, which of course was blue, as well as the moment I threw my bouquet to the single ladies in attendance, all four of them. I didn't throw the real one. I kept it for weeks and weeks until nothing in it was alive and it started to smell. I just simply didn't want to part with it.

Our wedding day surpassed all of our expectations. On this perfectly perfect Sunday I became his and he became mine. And, we are living happily ever after.

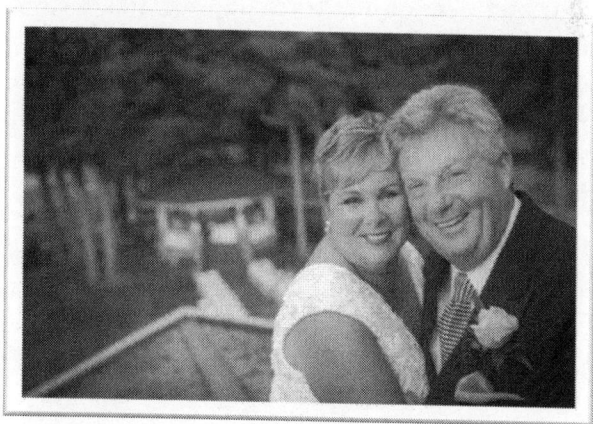

# The End... or so I thought

## 54 – You Can't Predict a Miracle

When I began to write this book, I could never have predicted how it would end. The goal was to share the story of the truly wonderful man I loved, Dennis, whose life had spiraled downward. Addiction is caused by unresolved grief (and in Dennis's case guilt as well), and the inability to resolve it. The pain in his life continued to cause more pain because it was never, ever talked about. After turning things around and having reached the happiest point in his life, cancer took him quickly. To me there was an underlying message about consequences. We make decisions for ourselves and others in our life and people make decisions for us, but no one thinks about the future and how those decisions will affect everyone involved. That was the story.

When I began writing I didn't have a clue what the future had in store for me. After Dennis had passed and at the time I started writing, a future husband was not on the horizon. In fact, that was the last thing I wanted. I wrote in fits and starts over nine years; with long periods in between inspiration and motivation. There were many days when writing about it became more difficult than living through it. Then the pain and secrets I held inside for so many years suddenly started to unleash my voice. Once Doug and I met and were married, I really looked forward to writing my happily-ever-after chapter and fully expected it to be my final one. At last, a chapter that really did have that happy ending. Then a miracle happened, and you certainly can't predict those. One of the biggest miracles in my life occurred right after writing some of the most difficult chapters in this book.

In the spring of 2018, I had just completed chapters 12 and 13. They had been terribly painful for me to write. Some days Doug, who was my greatest supporter, would hold me tightly while I cried my heart out. It was the Easter weekend and a friend offered us her condo in Victoria for a weekend getaway, and I really needed a break. On the Saturday morning, as I have done for forty-five years, I read the *Winnipeg Free Press* obituaries. It was a ritual that I now had access to online. On this particular morning there was a name I recognized, and it stopped me in my tracks.

In the mid '80s Dennis received a letter from a lawyer advising him that his ex-wife had remarried. Her new husband wished to adopt John and change his last name. Of course, Dennis had no objection and called his ex to offer his support, telling her that he was as near as the closest phone should she ever need him.

On this particular Saturday morning the name I read in the obituaries was that of John's adopted grandmother. I read on. It mentioned grandson John, his wife Katherine and great grandson Jacob. I thought my head would explode. John would now be fifty years of age. He had a wife and a son. His son would have been Dennis's grandson. His grandmother, the obituary said, was French and Catholic, and in that moment my heart broke again. John's real birth grandmother was also French and Catholic. The grandmother he never knew was an incredible woman who was the best mother-in-law I could have ever had. She died in 1986, having not seen her grandson John since he was two years old. If only we could go back and rewrite our history... but we can't. That's when I decided enough was enough. I had to do something, but what?

I took the counsel of two of my smartest girlfriends who reminded me that not all stories of this nature have a happy ending. I was also reminded again that this wasn't my story, but my children's story. John was the half-brother they never knew. After four sleepless nights I called both my children and put it in their hands. I told them the time and place of the funeral and if they wanted to reach out and make contact with John, they now had the opportunity. I also made the decision not to question them again. If they wanted to tell me what their decision was it would have to come from them.

A month later I was visiting Keele and had already been there for five days. It was just after dinner and we were sitting on the couch chatting. Without warning she simply said, "We've heard from John." I jumped up from the couch in shock and I started to shake and tear up. I could hardly believe what she said. Both my children agreed it was time to reach out. They composed a letter and put it into a sympathy card which my Damien delivered to the funeral home. After the funeral it was given to John. He reached out to them immediately. A forty-eight-year prayer had been answered!

Plans had been made in the previous six months for my daughter, who is a tremendous athlete, to do the Ironman triathlon in Whistler, BC at the end of July. In our family, when you turn nine years old, you get to go on a trip with your grandma. So, the nine-year-old twins and their eleven-year-old sister didn't know it, but I had booked an Alaskan cruise as a surprise, following the race. They would travel to Vancouver two days early and meet up with John and hopefully his family. I would meet up with them on the second day and hoped that somehow I could meet John as well, even if it was for five minutes. For the next two months my head was spinning, and my heart was filled with hope, but I had one giant fear.

I had only seen one photo of John when he was about two years old. Around 1979, when I worked for a large cosmetics company, I was in a department store and saw John and his mother. He was just a young boy and I recognized his mother from photographs my sister-in-law had. This was the first and only time I would see John in person, and he looked so identical to Dennis that the next thing I knew I was on the floor being revived by the store staff. I had passed out cold.

It was now July 2018. Dennis, who had died at the age of fifty-three, had been gone eighteen years. John was now fifty and I was absolutely terrified that he would still look like his father. To me that would be like seeing a ghost.

My daughter arrived in Vancouver and met John for drinks. The next day Keele and the kids went sightseeing, while I took the ferry from the island, then drove through Vancouver to meet up with her. We finally connected in her hotel room at 10 p.m. at night. John made the decision to go to Whistler with his ten-year-old son so he could see her in the big race. I offered to take everyone out for dinner on Saturday night.

John really didn't even know I existed, but for the thirty years I was married to Dennis he was always the third person in the room. His presence was always felt even though he wasn't there. This wasn't the young boy I had envisioned; he was a grown man with a son of his own, and I couldn't even imagine how either of us would feel upon meeting. I meant nothing to him, but he means the world to me. Although I had not seen John since he was a child, I'd regularly Googled his name ever since Google was invented. I knew what field his career was in and what city he lived in, but nothing else. I even put Dennis's obituary in the Vancouver newspaper when he died. I knew John was there and I hoped he would see it. Now that there was a possibility of meeting the man, I was an emotional wreck.

John had made a dinner reservation at a lovely Italian restaurant in Whistler. When he walked up the steps to greet us, I opened my arms wide and welcomed him into a giant hug. I said, with tremendous joy, "I've waited forty-eight years for this moment, and I'm buying dinner because I've waited forty-eight years to feed you." That broke the ice and the entire evening for me was like a dream. The location, dinner and wine were perfect, and it was delightful to have the four children with us. Afterward we all walked back to our condo and made plans for the next day.

John has his father's eyes and premature greying hair, and that's where the comparison ended. He is his own person—handsome, interesting, enthused and accomplished. His ten-year-old son, who would have also been my grandchild had history been different, was a perfect match for my three grandchildren. My grandson Jase is the only boy in two families, and now he has real boy cousin, and they all get along famously.

I spent most of Sunday afternoon with John, his son and my three grandchildren at his hotel pool while my daughter was in the twelve-hour Ironman. He's a wonderful dad and it is very obvious how important his son is to him. That Sunday was a chance to get to know him better.

And at last, I had an answer to the question I'd wondered about for eighteen years. Why did a Tarot card reader insist that the best place for me was Victoria, on Vancouver Island? Once I met Doug, I really thought he was the reason, but it was that weekend I learned that in

2000, and for the next several years, John had lived and worked in Victoria and that is where he met his wife. We could have crossed paths at any time and possibly did.

I would love to see John again, but I remind myself that I'm not related to him or a part of his life. What's important is the fact that all parties are excited about moving forward. He has found his siblings and they have at last found him. Because of the internet John knew he had a brother, but he didn't know he was also blessed with a sister. My greatest joy at dinner that first evening was seeing the way he looked at my beautiful daughter Keele. I could see in his eyes, and by the way that he looked at her, that he knew he'd won the sister lottery.

And, finally, in that precious moment my heart was forever healed.

# Acknowledgements

They say that it takes a village to raise a child, but I think it takes more than a village to write a book, for it is something you cannot do alone.

To my husband Doug: Without you this never would have happened. When we met, I had one chapter written and couldn't imagine that it would ever become a book. It was your constant encouragement and belief in my ability that kept me going on many a dark day. I love you like crazy!

To my dear friends and first readers: Mary Ann Amiss, Linda Stewart, Esther Gigliotti, Sandy McMullen and Gary O'Shaughnessy—you undertook the giant task of reading and correcting my errors while I took off on a two-month holiday. Thank you for your input, ideas and opinions and for making my first big step an easy one.

To Mary Ann Halpin: Photographer extraordinaire who caught my attention and made me fearless, I thank you.
Photography:
http://www.maryannhalpin.com
323-868-5692
Maryann@maryannhalpin.com

Jennifer Kaddoura was my editor for early-manuscript evaluation. Thank you for challenging me over and over, for your attention to detail and for helping me say what I needed to say and not what I wanted to.
Jennifer Kaddoura, Editor
Website: www.EditMeBrilliant.ca

My copy editor Nowick Gray was meant to be. Thank you for so easily getting me to the finish line. You have the knowledge and experience that made that last step seamless.
www.hyperedits.com

The design for my book cover was extremely important to me. My sincere thanks to Jeff Minkevics for taking my idea and adding your own talent and creativity which allowed me to have exactly what I envisioned.
Cover Copyright © 2020 by Jeff Minkevics

## Thank you for reading!

If you enjoyed this book, I hope you will share your experience with other readers by leaving a few comments at the bottom of the book's Amazon page, or by email to adele@bugsplat.ca (for book comments only).

Made in the USA
Columbia, SC
09 August 2022